THE FIRST EMPEROR'S WARRIORS

QIN SHI HUANGDI FIRST SOVEREIGN QIN EMPEROR

ISBN 0-9513032-1-X

Photosetting by Team.
Text set in
Berkeley Old Style.
Printed in Great Britain
by Balding + Mansell
UK Limited.

Our grateful thanks to the Ministry of Culture
in Beijing, People's Republic of China and the
Shaanxi Archaeological Overseas Exhibition
Corporation in Shaanxi, People's Republic of
China for kindly providing photographs used
extensively in this publication.

CONTENTS

■

THE FIRST EMPEROR'S WARRIORS

Undoubtedly the archaeological discovery of our time, the tomb of the First Emperor of China at Mount Li offers direct evidence for an historical event of the greatest importance; namely, the foundation of an empire that lasted from 221 B.C. until 1912.

The soldiers upon whom the terracotta warriors were modelled brought about this critical event in world history. In doing so, they elevated one prince to a position hitherto unknown in East Asia. A result was the elaborate preparations which the First Emperor undertook for his own safety in the after-life: most incredible of all was the making of a life-sized underground army.

The author has written several books on Chinese civilisation, including *The First Emperor of China* and *China, A Concise Cultural History.* The latter is being published in early 1988 by John Murray and the New American Library. His study of the Qin dynasty has been assisted by the Chinese authorities, who in 1980 invited the Cotterell family to visit the excavations at Mount Li. The translations in this study of the terracotta army are provided by his wife, Yong Yap Cotterell, whose own published works include *The Chinese Kitchen* and *Wok Magic.*

ARTHUR COTTERELL

DESIGNED AND COMPILED BY THE BUTTON DESIGN COMPANY

Susan Bingham · Gill Topping · Joseph Mills · Andrew Newman · Andrew Murray · Martyn Woodhouse · Maria Macey

THE DISCOVERY OF THE TERRACOTTA
ARMY AT MOUNT LI

Although Chinese tradition contains a hint of the magnificence with which the First Emperor was laid to rest in 210 B.C., its account of the tomb at Mount Li makes no reference to the incredible underground army that was designed to protect this ruler in the after-life. Archaeologists were quite unprepared for the 1974 discovery of a detachment of terracotta warriors. Local farmers who were digging a well that year accidentally broke into part of a pit containing more than 6,000 life-sized figures.

Excavation of this initial find, termed Pit No. 1, has now revealed an armoured infantry unit on the point of throwing

itself upon the First Emperor's enemies. Situated about one and a half kilometres to the east of the tumulus, the force was obviously intended to guard the eastern entrance to the site of the tomb. Further investigation also disclosed in 1976 two other underground chambers filled with terracotta warriors. One of them, Pit No. 2, contains a regiment of chariots and cavalry, with some unmounted support; there are estimated to be 1,400 warriors and 90 chariots altogether. The final detachment of the terracotta army was buried in Pit No. 3, a small chamber which was fully explored in the ensuing year. The ceremonial weapons recovered, and the large number of officers amongst its 68 figures, would seem to indicate that this was the position where the commander-in-chief stood.

The importance of these discoveries was recognised at once. The site became the focus of intense archaeological activity and great care was taken in the reconstruction and preservation of the terracotta figures themselves. Today Pit No. 1 is still being meticulously restored beneath a hangar-like roof which has been designed to withstand the earthquakes so prevalent in Shaanxi province.

The detail of the men and horses remains the amazing feature of the site. Not only can we observe the construction of body armour, with even the heads of rivets standing out, but more the soles of the shoes worn by kneeling soldiers display a definite tread pattern. It is this accuracy that makes the warriors of the terracotta army so valuable: they provide direct material evidence for our understanding of the greatest event in the history of China, the unification of the country as an empire. We are afforded a privileged glimpse of the Imperial Guard, the crack soldiers of the invincible army of Qin. From this unexpected sight it is possible to appreciate the nature of "the long whip" which, the Histories tell us, the First Emperor used "to drive the world before him, swallow up the land, and overthrow the feudal lords."

*The armoured
infantry unit of
Pit No. 1.*

*A corridor in Pit No. 1,
before restoration.*

An empty fourth pit suggests that the terracotta army was incomplete on the fall of the Qin dynasty in 206 B.C. But, even if the three underground chambers containing warriors were all that archaeologists had discovered at Mount Li, the First Emperor's mausoleum would be justly famous. For the individual portraiture executed by the potter-sculptors who modelled the warriors' heads is in itself fascinating. A degree of standardisation is apparent in the treatment of the torso, but each detachable soldier's head is unique: no two heads have been found to be alike, and easily recognisable are individual personalities as well as the various physical types of the Chinese empire.

It might even be said that these personal portraits celebrate the unification of "all under Heaven," the drawing together in a single state all the different groups who originally constituted the Chinese nation. Since the ancient Chinese were never a homogeneous people, membership depended on a common cultural heritage rather than ethnic affinity. At the centre of the culture was ancestor worship: the deceased ancestors, in particular those of kings, had to be propitiated with elaborate rites. As absolute ruler, the First Emperor obviously intended that his cult should set the pattern for imperial ancestor worship.

Recent excavation close to the tumulus has caused a reassessment of the whole site. Because one of the biggest projects undertaken by the First Emperor was the construction of his own tomb, it became a target of rebel wrath on the fall of the dynasty. Looting and damage by fire was the lot of much of the terracotta army, but the discovery in 1980 of an undisturbed pit of bronze chariots next to the western edge of the tumulus shows that rebel destruction in 206 B.C. was less thorough than contemporary accounts in the Histories state. Quite possibly the burial chamber of the First Emperor could also be in the condition in which it was sealed up four years before.

One of the bronze chariots excavated to the west of the tumulus in 1980.

*Amongst the
terracotta warriors
no two heads are
alike.*

Although somewhat damaged by the collapse of the timbers supporting the pit roof, the bronze chariots provide crucial technical information, as the wooden vehicles stationed with the terracotta army have long since crumbled away. Their non-military function is apparent from the decorations on the sides and roof of each chariot, and so they may have been intended for the use of the imperial household, or even the First Emperor himself.

The unexpected discovery of the bronze chariot pit has rekindled interest in the progress of the work at Mount Li. Clearly funeral arrangements were more advanced than the emptiness of Pit No. 4 of the terracotta army at first led archaeologists to believe. It is not impossible that there will be announcements of more pits in the future; yet few of these new finds are likely to eclipse the splendour of the terracotta army, if only for the reason that the scale of its execution leaves little scope for serious competition. The 7,000 figures already known to be buried at Mount Li make this section of the mausoleum a discovery unmatched in world archaeology.

Remains of a wooden chariot.

Whether or not other discoveries take place, within the tumulus or its environs, the pace of their subsequent excavation will be measured. There is indeed a commendable reluctance not to rush the job. During the summer of 1980, when the bronze chariots were discovered, I was at Mount Li as a guest of the Chinese authorities. It was in conversation there with the archaeologists that a difference in attitude to history became so apparent. No sense of urgency prevailed on the site and no immediate plans were being laid to open the tumulus, the curator Yang Chen Ching even joking that its excavator might well be his own grandson. This deliberate slowness rests on a profound awareness of cultural continuity, on an intimate connection with the past. What Yang Chen Ching did not need to say was that just as his ancestors had buried the First Emperor so his descendants were bound to dig him up. As members of the only civilisation that has endured uninterrupted from ancient times, the Chinese have a time-scale of their own. It is therefore appropriate that in the current excavations at Mount Li they are investigating the greatest archaeological site ever found.

Vanguard of Pit No. 1, showing the three ranks of crossbowmen.

Infantrymen as found in Pit No. 1.

QIN SHI HUANGDI,
THE FIRST EMPEROR OF CHINA

The First Emperor.

The person who built the mausoleum at Mount Li was Zheng, king of Qin from 246 B.C. and all China after 221 B.C. The sweeping victories that his troops gained over the armies of rival kings brought about the unification of the country and his elevation as the First Emperor. That he chose to have the best of these men reproduced life size in clay for service in the after-life is perhaps an indication of where he believed his essential strength to lie.

Whilst Zheng did not lead his forces in person, he kept very strict control over the movements of each unit. So tight was the command structure in the Qin army that none of his generals would accept orders as valid unless they were accompanied by imperial tallies. Made in the form of a tiger, they were divided down the middle into two sections. Those tallies which have survived refer to specific regiments, usually called "armoured forces." Strong central authority had always been typical of the state Zheng ruled, but during his reign the power of the throne knew no limits and opposition was not tolerated from any quarter.

After the final victory in 221 B.C. over Qi, one of the oldest states in China, the military despotism of Qin became transparent to all. In the end, the bullying administration of the first imperial dynasty the Chinese people had ever experienced, gave rise to a rebellion that devastated the country in a prolonged civil war. So fundamental were the changes the First Emperor introduced, however, that the mere fifteen years the house of Qin reigned supreme represent a watershed in the history of China. The attempt to re-establish the feudal states which the Qin army had crushed was a miserable failure, and a unified empire came to seem an inevitable political development. But it is possible that the founder of the next dynasty, the Han, received such an enthusiastic welcome from the Chinese people because of his humble origins. They had had enough of absolute princes.

Imperial tally used
to communicate
orders to units of
the Qin army.

The unprecedented position of Zheng as ruler of "all under Heaven" certainly encouraged despotism. At this stage in history, China was unaware of any other civilisations in the world. To the north of the Yellow river was the barren steppe, whose nomadic inhabitants compelled the building of the defensive barriers soon to be incorporated in the First Emperor's Great Wall; to the east was the largest ocean in which lay the primitive islands of Japan; to the west the highest mountain system blocked trade routes to India and West Asia; while southwards were semi-tropical forests where rudimentary cultivators lagged behind in cultural achievement. Well over a millennium of civilised living had already passed by the time the country was unified by the Qin army. And yet another century was to elapse, before in 126 B.C. the first envoy was to return from a mission to the western nomads with the startling news that in what is now Afghanistan there were "cities, mansions and houses as in China."

Even then the difficult overland journey via the oasis towns of Central Asia kept outside contact down to a minimum. But during the reign of the First Emperor (221– 210 B.C.) there was no inkling of the existence of India at all, let alone any other ancient centre of civilisation. It is hardly surprising therefore that the concentration of wealth, prestige and authority about a single person led to expectations hitherto unknown in China.

Was not Zheng the greatest ruler who had ever lived? Was it not fitting that his tomb as well as his palace should reflect this novel status? Hence, the grandeur with which the imperial capital at Xianyang was laid out: the First Emperor's city was the exact counterpart of the Great Wall, the only work of mankind that is visible to an astronaut.

Awareness of the singular destiny enjoyed by Zheng is evident in the discussions which the Histories record taking place on the capitulation of Qi. Because "the unification of the land was something never achieved before," the question of the imperial title was considered at length in the Qin court. Ministers consulted learned men about the titles used by earlier monarchs and finally recommended Supreme Sovereign. Whereupon Zheng announced: "Supreme may be ignored but Sovereign adopted along with the ancient title of Emperor. We are to be called the First Emperor, and our successors known as the Second Emperor, Third Emperor, and so on, for endless generations." This choice was one of the great ironies of history, as the Qin dynasty was to end with the second generation.

Nonetheless, Zheng showed an important side of his character in selecting the title Qin Shi Huangdi, First Sovereign Qin Emperor, for he was asserting more than a supremacy over the other kings he had dethroned. The word for emperor (di) in the title almost certainly contained the idea of divinity. Already a very old and complex form of address in 221 B.C., it had always been used for major dieties, and especially the founder-ancestors of legendary dynasties. Daoist thinkers attributed superhuman qualities to those who bore the title, such as the mythical Yellow Emperor, Huang Di. Zheng could not have been ignorant of the manner of the Yellow Emperor's departure: after giving his kingdom an orderliness previously unknown on earth, Huang Di rose into the sky as an immortal.

The first occasion on which the First Emperor tried to make contact with the Immortals was in 219 B.C., when ambassadors were sent to request the elixir of life. During the remaining nine years of his reign, several embassies were dispatched to the tops of mountains, then thought to be the abodes of those who were "aged but undying." An expedition "with several thousand boys and girls" was even sent across the Yellow Sea in order to find the Isles of the Immortals. It did not return.

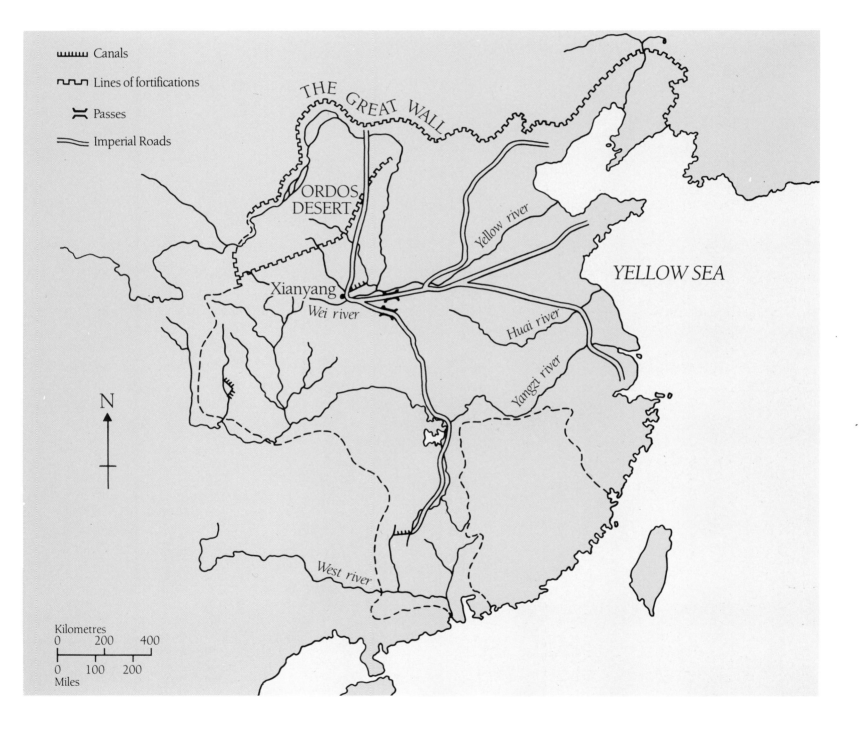

Canals

Lines of fortifications

Passes

Imperial Roads

THE GREAT WALL

ORDOS DESERT

Xianyang

Wei river

Yellow river

YELLOW SEA

Huai river

Yangzi river

N

West river

Kilometres
0   200   400

0   100   200
Miles

The Qin empire
(221 – 206 B.C.)

While Daoist magicians conducted officials on these unusual diplomatic ventures, and other experts sought to miraculously produce gold, the First Emperor also commissioned a tomb which archaeology today is revealing to be one of the wonders of the world. It is interesting to observe how his anxiety about the after-life caused such a massive diversion of resources to its construction. Although planned as early as 246 B.C., after unification the mausoleum became the major project undertaken in the empire, since the 700,000 conscripts who toiled at Mount Li were twice the number used for the building of the Great Wall.

The First Emperor, according to the Histories, "was a man of great intellect and force of character, but he was exceedingly superstitious and in constant dread of death." An interview with a Daoist adept in 212 B.C. provides a telling insight of both weaknesses. We are told how a certain Lu reported:

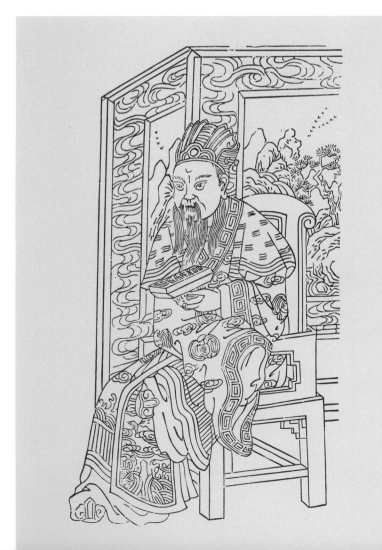

"Our search for magic fungus, rare herbs and immortal beings has come to nothing. It seems that a sinister influence was against us. It is my sincere opinion that Your Majesty would be well advised to change quarters secretly from time to time, in order to avoid evil spirits; for in their absence some pure being will surely come. For subjects to have knowledge of their sovereign's whereabouts detracts from his divinity. An Immortal is one who cannot be wet by water or burned by fire, who rides on the clouds and air and who endures as long as Heaven and earth. Since he who governs the empire cannot live a pure, simple life, we hope Your Majesty will not let it be known in which palace you are staying. Then, we shall be able to obtain the elixir of life."

On hearing of this impediment to his greatest wish, immortality, the First Emperor said that in future he would no longer use the royal We; on the contrary, he would only refer to himself as a pure being. He issued more practical instructions too. "The two hundred and seventy palaces and pavilions within 200 *li* of Xianyang were to be connected by causeways and covered walks and furnished with hangings, bells, drums and beautiful women, each at the appropriate place. Disclosure of his whereabouts was made punishable by death."

How determined the First Emperor was to facilitate the quest for an elixir became clear straightaway. From one of his residences, he observed the approach of his chief adviser Li Si (280–208 B.C.) commenting adversely on the size of the minister's retinue. One of the palace eunuchs informed Li Si, who reduced the number of his retainers. This action so angered the First Emperor that he had all the eunuchs in his company executed, since none would admit to telling tales. "After this," the Histories noted, "his movements were kept secret, but it was always in the Xianyang palace that he conducted state business."

*Grand Councillor
Li Si.*

The Great Wall of China.

Yet easily influenced though he was by anyone who professed to be informed about the supernatural, the circumstances of Zheng's own life before he mounted the imperial throne undoubtedly encouraged a quest for personal security. When he came to the throne of Qin in 246 B.C., he was only thirteen years old. The actual ruler for many years was the ex-merchant Lu Buwei, who had snatched Zheng's father from obscurity and secured his accession. Although Lu Buwei was an able minister and strategist, his regency was personally disastrous for the young king, because in 238– 237 B.C. Zheng's own mother was implicated in a plot against the throne. The rebels were crushed, but Zheng felt obliged to banish Lu Buwei who later killed himself in 235 B.C. and to place the queen mother under house arrest.

Anti-Qin sentiment has embroidered these events, so that Zheng's mother is portrayed in most accounts as little more than a shameless whore. Although she was originally the concubine of Lu Buwei, there is no evidence to suggest that once he passed her over to the admiring prince, she was anything but a loyal wife. Having backed the father of the future First Emperor, it is unlikely that Lu Buwei would have jeopardised the special position he had acquired by continuing a relationship with his ex-concubine. The charge that he sired Zheng can therefore be regarded as an attempt to besmirch the latter's name. In a society that revered ancestors the insult of being the bastard son of a mere trader could not have been worse. Stories about "the grave immoralities" committed by Zheng's mother later on are probably further invention, although it is true that her son was obliged to "shut her up in a strong fortress" after the rebellion of 238–237 B.C.

Whatever the truth behind the sombre events of his youth, they made Zheng mistrustful, and opened the way for authoritarianism forever associated with the name of the First Emperor. And, as we have seen, they also brought about a preoccupation with immortality which in the final years of his reign was to leave state affairs dangerously in the hands of a few advisers. After 212 B.C. the First Emperor seems to have relied almost entirely on Li Si and the eunuch Zhao Gao.

But in the period after his assumption of full power in Qin, Zheng was particularly attracted by the harsh dictatorship then being advocated by Han Fei Zi (280–233 B.C.). A leading thinker of the so-called School of Law, Han Fei Zi praised only those occupations that contributed to the military efficiency of the state. To direct all the energies of the state towards the war effort, cruel punishments were required. Han Fei Zi argued that it had to be made worse for people to fall into the hands of the police than to fight the forces of an enemy state. Single-mindedness on the part of the ruler, he asserted in an essay entitled *The Five Lice*, was essential.

To reward those who cut off the heads of the enemy, and yet admire acts of mercy and compassion; to give out titles and money to those who capture the enemy's cities, and yet listen to doctrines of universal love; to improve one's armour and weapons in preparation for the time of trouble, and yet desire the elegant attire of the leisured gentry; to hope to enrich the state through agriculture and ward off the enemy with trained soldiers, and yet pay honour to literary men; to ignore those people who respect their rulers and fear the law, and instead favour bands of wandering knights – to indulge in contradictory and pointless acts like these is to ensure that the state will never be well ordered. Whilst a state at peace may patronize scholars and knights, a state at war must rely solely upon its fighting men. So, those who are of real profit to the state are not used and those who are used are of no profit. So it is that those who attend to government business are careless in their posts and wandering scholars increase in number day by day. From all this arises the disorder of the age.

When Zheng read *The Five Lice*, he exclaimed: "If I could once meet of its author and converse with him, I should die without regret."

*The tumulus of the
First Emperor.*

21

The meeting took place in 233 B.C., but proved fatal for the philosopher, not the king. At the suggestion of Zheng's chief adviser, Li Si, an army had been prepared for an attack on the state of Han, a bitter enemy of Qin. Li Si told Zheng that by seizing Han he would terrify all the other states. On the eve of the Qin invasion, the Han king sent Han Fei Zi to Zheng's court as a friendly ambassador. One account relates

how the Qin king was delighted with the philosopher, but he did not yet trust him enough to use his counsel. So Li Si . . . did him injury and slandered him, saying, 'Han Fei Zi is a prince of Han. At present Your Highness wishes to annex the lands of the feudal lords. Han Fei Zi is bound to side with Han. Such is human nature . . . The best thing to do is to hand him over to the law officers for investigation.' King Zheng assented to this . . . Li Si then sent a man secretly to Han Fei Zi carrying poison. Unable to obtain an interview with the king in order to state his case, Han Fei Zi was induced to poison himself. Later the Qin king felt regret and sent an official to release the philosopher, but by that time only a corpse remained.

The motives of Li Si are unfathomable. He had arranged the death of a man who had once been his fellow student, who was an emissary, and with whose views he himself was in accord. Possibly the two men were rivals from student days. Tradition has it that Li Si considered himself inferior to Han Fei Zi. In the cut and thrust of the Qin court Li Si may have felt that his own position was insufficiently secure to tolerate the presence of such an eminent adviser to the crown. The future Grand Councillor of the Qin empire could well have been as ambitious for power as his young master. Whatever reason lay behind the trick, the irony is that as a result of it the most dictatorial ruler of ancient China allowed the destruction of the sternest spokesman of totalitarianism.

Death almost visited Zheng himself in 227 B.C., as a result of the constant encroachment of his army on the territory of other states. Even distant Yan felt so threatened that its crown prince devised a plan to rid China of the Qin king. This nobleman tried to persuade the scholar-swordsman Jing Ke to tackle the difficult task with these words:

"Qin has an avaricious heart and its desires are insatiable. It will not be satisfied till it has subjugated the kings of all the lands within the Four Seas. Qin has already taken the Han ruler prisoner and annexed all his territory. It has furthermore raised troops to attack Chu in the south and overawe Zhao in the north . . .

Zhao cannot resist Qin and must accept its overlordship. If this comes to pass, then Yan will be overtaken by disaster. Yan is small and weak, and has often suffered from war. Were our entire population conscripted, the levy would be insufficient to oppose Qin. The feudal lords are submissive to Qin, and none dare join a grand alliance against it.

My secret plan is to find one of the world's brave men and send him to Qin, where he could play on King Zheng's greed. With his strength, he would certainly achieve our aim. If he could actually succeed in kidnapping the Qin king and force him to return his gains to the feudal lords . . . that would be splendid. But if this were not possible, he could use the opportunity to stab and kill him . . . Then the feudal lords could unite, and their defeat of Qin would be assured."

After some hesitation, Jing Ke accepted the commission but he was at a loss to think of a way to gain an audience with Zheng. Meanwhile the advance of Qin to the borders of Yan, following the annexation of the neighbouring state of Zhao, caused the crown prince to urge immediate action. Yet not even the fear he felt about Qin ambitions was sufficient to make him accept the ruse that Jing Ke cleverly hit upon. The scholar-swordwman suggested that he take as a present to Zheng the head of a fugitive Qin general for whom a very large reward had already been posted. As Jing Ke correctly guessed that the crown prince would never violate the laws of

A stone relief showing Jing Ke's attempted assassination of Zheng in 227 B.C.

hospitality and order the defector's execution, he boldly approached the ex-general and outlined his plan to him. Recalling the merciless killing of his own kin, this man told Jing Ke that "day and night he had been grinding his teeth and beating his breast"; whereupon he willingly accepted "his instructions" and cut his own throat.

Once the crown prince heard of this sacrifice, he rushed to the corpse and mourned with deep grief. "But the deed was done," the Histories comment, "and so the head was put into a container. Then the crown prince purchased one of the world's sharp daggers and had an artisan impregnate it with a terrible poison." Thus equipped with the head, a map showing a gift of territory, and the poisoned dagger, Jing Ke set off for Xianyang accompanied by a Yan bravado named Qin Wuyang. As expected, Zheng was eager to give an audience, once he heard of the apparent submission of Yan. He even "put on full ceremonial clothing as for a great state occasion, and commanded that the emissary be received in the audience chamber of the Xianyang palace." In the court therefore,

Jing Ke approached to present the head . . . followed by Qin Wuyang, presenting the container with the map. When they came to the steps of the throne, Qin Wuyang changed colour and trembled fearfully. The courtiers being amazed at this behaviour, Jing Ke said: "He is a common man of the northern peoples, and has never seen the Son of Heaven. Therefore he shakes with fear. May it please Your Majesty to excuse him for a while and allow me your humble servant, to advance."

On being instructed to do so, Jing Ke took out the map, unrolled it, and exposed the dagger. Seizing the sleeve of the Qin king with his left hand, Jing Ke grasped the dagger with the right and struck at him. In alarm King Zheng leapt backwards so that his sleeve tore off. Though he tried hard, the king was unable to draw his sword,

which was very long . . . Jing Ke pursued the king, who ran around a pillar. The astounded courtiers were simply paralysed.

In Qin law a courtier was forbidden to carry weapons. Moreover the royal guard was not allowed to enter the audience chamber unless summoned. At this critical moment there was not time to call for the soldiers anyway. Thus Jing Ke chased King Zheng, who overcome by panic tried to ward off the dagger blows with his two joined hands.

At this juncture the court physician, one Xia Wuzu struck Jing Ke with his medicine bag. King Zheng, however, continued to dash round and round the pillar, so distraught was he. Then a courtier cried out: "Put your sword behind you, King!" By doing so, he found he could unsheathe the weapon and wound Jing Ke in the left thigh. Disabled, Jing Ke raised his dagger and hurled it at the king, but it missed and hit a bronze pillar. King Zheng then wounded his assailant seven more times.

Realizing his attempt had failed, Jing Ke leaned against a pillar and with a laugh said, "I failed because I wanted to capture you alive. Someone else will now have to serve the crown prince." Then it was that they killed the scholar-swordsman.

This brush with death marked Zheng, who "was not at ease for a long time." Except of Xia Wuzu, whom he rewarded with gold, his courtiers had not rallied to the defence. Anger and fear filled his thoughts, deepening a sense of isolation that first arose when he learned of his mother's betrayal. While Zheng threw himself into campaigns against rival kings down till 221 B.C. and the thorough reorganisation of China after unification, the psychological impact of Jing Ke's attack was reinforced by two other violent assaults. In 219 B.C. a blind musician tried to strike the First Emperor at court with a lead-filled harp; then a year later a third would-be assassin ambushed the wrong carriage on one of the imperial tours of the provinces.

The reformed script of Qin, possibly by Li Si himself.

Apart from increasing his dread of dying and spurring on fruitless searches for a drug of immortality, these dangerous encounters led to Zheng's final aloofness from all but a small circle of advisers. The First Emperor became a remote ruler, preoccupied with his own destiny as the Son of Heaven. It was an attitude of mind that indirectly ruined the Qin dynasty, since in 210 B.C. his death could be kept from public knowledge long enough to eliminate the heir-apparent Fu Su, whom Li Si feared. As a result, a worthless younger son was installed as the Second Emperor and the oppressed Chinese people had their chance to revolt.

Without doubt the First Emperor's anxiety about dying was exploited by the Daoist adepts and magicians whom he summoned to Xianyang. But it would seem that Zheng genuinely believed he had attained his eminence through the exercise of his own talents. The absolute power vested in him was both the outcome of his own energy and the sign of divine approval. Although he was fortunate to possess in Li Si such an able Grand Councillor, the determination of Zheng was patently the driving force behind the Qin juggernaut, as even critical passages in the Histories bear witness. Speaking of the conditions at court in 212 B.C., the Daoist scholar Lu said to a colleague:

The First Emperor is stubborn and self-willed. Starting as prince in one state, he conquered the whole empire, and now that all his ambitions are fulfilled he thinks no one since time immemorial can compare with him. He relies solely on the law officers, whom he trusts. Although there are seventy court scholars, their posts are ornamental because he does not heed their advice. The prime minister and other high officials only deal with routine matters, leaving all to the throne. The First Emperor loves to intimidate men with punishments and death, so that to avoid being charged with disloyalty officials dare not speak out. The ruler, who never has his faults condemned, is growing prouder and prouder while those below him cringe in fear and try to please him with flattery and lies.

According to the law of the land, no man may practise two arts and anyone who fails in his task may be executed. No less than 300 astrologers are watching the stars, but these good men, for fear of giving offence, merely flatter the First Emperor and dare not speak of his faults. It is he who decides all affairs of state, great and small. He even has the documents weighed every morning and night, and will not rest until a certain weight has passed through his hands. How can we find herbs of immortality for such a tyrant?"

The sudden departure of Lu, along with other experts in this field of research, caused the First Emperor to purge the scholars in the capital. Some 460 were killed despite opposition from his eldest son Fu Su, who argued that the killings would unsettle the population. "I collected all the writings of the empire and destroyed those which were of no use," the First Emperor fumed. "I assembled a host of learned men and alchemists to start a reign of peace, hoping that the alchemists would find marvellous herbs. But I have nothing to show for all the money spent and, even worse, now I find that scholars go about the capital saying how the throne lacks virtue."

A feeling of insecurity in the face of both natural and supernatural dangers began to haunt Zheng. He is once supposed to have said that he could observe to the south of Xianyang "an emanation of a Son of Heaven," which at the time was thought to be a mist red within and yellow without on all sides. Without success he endeavoured to apprehend this rival, who was later said to have been Liu Bang, the first emperor of the subsequent Han dynasty. The discovery in 211 B.C. of a meteorite – "a shooting star which changed into a stone" – worried Zheng enormously. When it was reported that someone had inscribed on the stone, "After Qin Shi Huangdi's death the land will be divided," he had all the people living in the neighbourhood slain and the stone pulverized. "Then the First Emperor," according to the Histories, "was unable to find happiness and so he ordered the composition of poems about the Immortals and had them sung each day."

*Terracotta warrior
in excavation in Pit
No. 1.*

*Charioteer from Pit
No. 1.*

In 210 B.C. Zheng died at the age of fifty, during one of his journeys through the eastern provinces, journeys which, though ostensibly tours of inspection, were really prolonged searches for immortality. Having had a dream of a sea-god interpreted as an evil spirit keeping him from contact with the Immortals, he roamed the northern shore of Shandong province until he dispatched what was most likely a whale with a repeater crossbow. Shortly afterwards the First Emperor sickened and died, but fearing for their lives Li Si and Zhao Gao suppressed the news and sent a forged edict ordering Fu Su and others whom they hated to commit suicide. Then they headed towards Xianyang and placed a cartload of mouldering fish directly in front of the imperial litter. "It was summer," the Histories dryly note, "and to disguise the stench of the corpse the escort was told to load a cart with salted fish." Because of the terror inspired by the imperial title, there was neither an onlooker to question the arrangements made for the homeward journey, nor on arrival in the capital was there an official to oppose the forged will which gave the throne to Hu Hai, the incompetent younger son.

*Head of an
unarmoured
crossbowman.*

THE TRIUMPH OF QIN AND THE UNIFICATION OF CHINA

The origins of the state of Qin date from the very end of the Early Zhou period (1027-771 B.C.). A civil war in 771 B.C. opened the way to a savage nomad attack on the city of Hao, near present-day Xi'an in Shaanxi province. The city was sacked through the alliance of barbarian tribesmen and the relations of the queen, who had been put aside because of the Zhou king's preference for a certain concubine. The king was killed but, with the aid of great vassals, the dynasty survived the catastrophe, although a new royal residence had to be established in a safer position at Luoyang, some distance down the Yellow river. Zhou prestige was shattered and power shifted to the great nobles who restored the dynasty. The abandoned territory around ruined Hao in the Wei river valley was awarded to a local chieftain, whose difficult task it was to safeguard the north-western frontier from renewed nomad incursions. From this local warlord descended Zheng, the First Emperor of China.

With the advantage of hindsight, Chinese historians concluded that this award of territory was the start of an unbroken chain of events that ended with the triumph of Qin in 221 B.C. They believed that "the very duties ennobled Qin would be called upon to perform would inevitably develop his ambition, for the military skills of his people could not but be improved by their constant struggles with raiding tribesmen along the frontier." It is easier for us to see today that the rise of Qin was as much the result of the effective use to which the natural resources of the Wei river valley were put as it was the undoubted military prowess of the Qin army.

Although Qin was to triumph over all the other feudal states in 221 B.C., and in doing so unify China as an empire, the struggle for supremacy was bitterly contested and by no means a foregone conclusion prior to Zheng's accession to the throne. Whilst the great lords all declared their loyalty to the restored Zhou monarch in 770 B.C., the throne was unable to

recover its former authority and considerable power had to be delegated to senior members of the nobility. Gradually this devolution left the Zhou kings with only a religious function and an impoverished royal domain surrounding Luoyang. Before the fourth century B.C. the rulers of the largest states were independent enough to style themselves kings (*wang*).

With the decay of feudal obligations and the undermining of the central role of the Zhou royal house, the emergent states fought each other for territory and competed to attract technicians and peasant-farmers. In the west primitive Qin encouraged immigration from rivals by offering houses and exemption from military service. Incessant warfare, either between the Chinese themselves or with invading barbarians from the northern steppes, brought about a substantial reduction in the number of states. According to the Histories, some 1,700 fiefs existed before 770 B.C. At the start of the seventh century B.C. there were only 200 feudal territories; by 500 B.C. that number had dropped to less than twenty. During the Warring States period (481-221 B.C.) the internecine struggle became so intense and so harsh that only seven states were able to concentrate adequate resources for war: these contestants were Qi, Yan, Zhao, Han, Wei, Chu and Qin. Powerless the Zhou monarch, the supposed Son of Heaven, watched as two great powers, Qin and Chu, still incompletely sinicized, gained territory through the quarrels of the older feudal states. The last Zhou king was dethroned by Qin troops in 256 B.C.

Prior to the triumph of Qin an alternative method of government was tried, the hegemon system (*ba*), which maintained a semblance of order until the fifth century B.C. The first hegemon was Huan, duke of Qi (684-642 B.C.). Though Qi's strength in what today is Shandong province was based on local sources of salt and iron, the elevation of its ruler to pre-eminence resulted from the energetic measures Huan took in dealing with barbarian incursions and inter-state

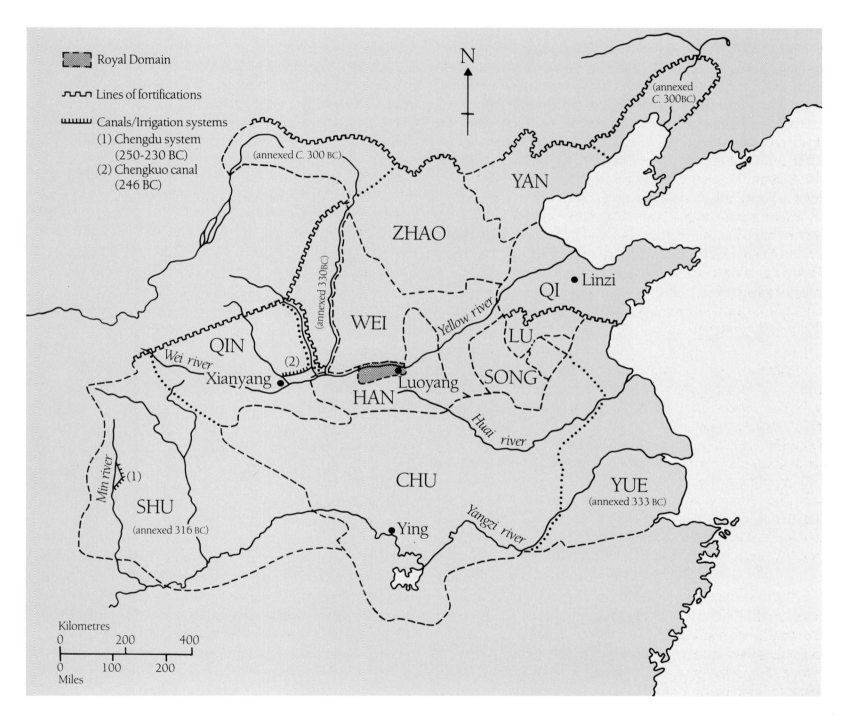

N

(annexed
C. 300BC)

(annexed C. 300 BC)

YAN

ZHAO

(annexed 330BC)

Linzi

QI

WEI

Yellow river

QIN

LU

Wei river

SONG

Xianyang

(2)

Luoyang

HAN

Huai river

Min river

(1)

CHU

YUE
(annexed 333 BC)

SHU

(annexed 316 BC)

Ying

Yangzi river

Kilometres
0   200   400

0   100   200
Miles

*Warring States
period (481 – 221
B.C.)*

rivalry. On the advice of his chief minister Guan Zong (died 645 B.C.), Huan called conferences to discuss matters of mutual interest and alliances were formed against truculent states. Signatories of agreements drawn up at these meetings were charged with punishing the unfilial, defending the principle of inheritance, honouring the worthy, respecting the aged, protecting children and strangers, choosing talented officials instead of relying on hereditary officers, abstaining from putting officials to death, and avoiding acts of provocation, such as the construction of barriers, the unannounced placing of boundary markers, and the restriction of the sale of grain. But these good intentions had to be backed by force: in the forty-two years Huan was hegemon he went to war no less than twenty-eight times.

Huan always claimed to act on behalf of the Son Heaven, but his actions were really directed by the needs of Qi. Later hegemons hardly bothered to cloak their intentions by any reference to the feudal obligations owed to the Zhou king. A family feud for the succession on Huan's death ruined Qi and allowed the hegemony to pass first to neighbouring Song, and then to Jin, the biggest state of all until internal troubles in 403 B.C. split it into three separate units: Han, Wei and Zhao. Jin included large parts of Shanxi, Hebei and Henan provinces, and its duke felt that he could afford to summon and dismiss the Son of Heaven without ceremony. A similar disregard for rank is evident in the intrigue and violence within the competing states themselves, a tendency which became very pronounced towards the end of the Warring States period. The last hegemon Zhuang, duke of Chu (613-591 B.C.), was taxed by difficulties both within and outside his state.

Before its disintegration into three separate states in 403 B.C., Jin was already threatened by two great rivals – Qin in the west and Chu in the south. Indeed, the struggle between these partly sinicised states was the dynamic behind the movement towards imperial unification. Of the two, Qin was best placed after the collapse of Jin, since there was little unity of purpose amongst the other northern states; while in the Yangzi estuary Chu had to deal with the belligerent powers of Yue and Wu. Not until 333 B.C. did Chu win a decisive victory over these states and secure its flank, by which time Qin had thoroughly reorganised itself under the guidance of Shang Yang (390-338 B.C.) and was ready to take the offensive. In 330 B.C. Qin extended its border to the Yellow river, at the expense of Wei, and in 316 B.C. a south-western thrust allowed the annexation of Shu, a large portion of modern Sichuan. Besides threatening Chu, the Shu conquest added valuable resources to Qin once the Min river scheme introduced irrigation to the Chengdu plain.

The Histories are not blind to the economic factor behind the apparently relentless Qin advance. Writing almost a century after the First Emperor's reign, the Han historian Sima Qian singles out "water benefits" as the critical development, although he points to the construction of Chengkuo canal as the turning point in the struggle. This opened in 246 B.C., the year of Zheng's accession to the throne. The proposal for the vast water-conservancy scheme came from the rival state of Han. Sima Qian relates

how the king of Han wished to prevent the eastern expansion of Qin by exhausting it with projects. He therefore sent the water engineer, Cheng Kuo, to the king of Qin to convince him that a canal should be built between the Jing and the Luo rivers. The proposed canal would be 300 li long and used for irrigation. The project was half finished when the plot was discovered. The Qin ruler was stopped from killing Cheng Kuo by the engineer's own argument. "Although this scheme was intended to injure you," he said, "if the canal is completed, it will bring great benefit to your state." The work was then ordered to be continued. When finished it irrigated 40,000 ching of poor land with water laden with rich silt. The productivity of the fields rose to one chung for each mu. Thus, the interior became a fertile plain without bad years. Qin then grew rich and strong and finally conquered all other feudal states. The canal was called after Cheng Kuo, who built it.

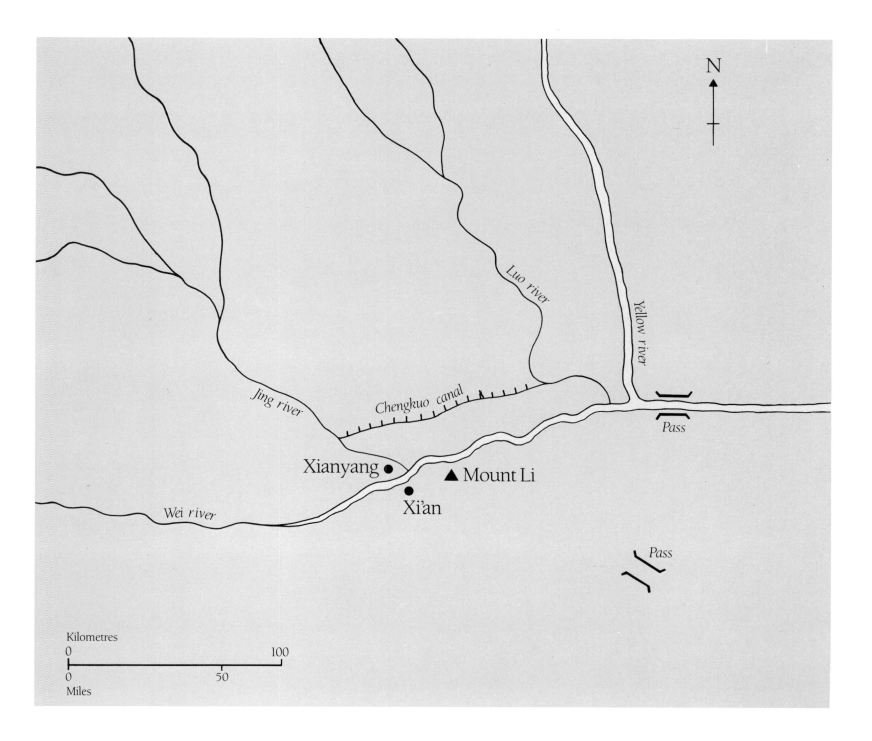

N

Luo river

Yellow river

Jing river

Chengkuo canal

Pass

Xianyang

▲ Mount Li

Xi'an

Wei river

Pass

Kilometres
0   100
0   50
Miles

Wei river valley.

The stratagem misfired badly: Han had bestowed on Qin the means of eventual victory. The additional grain from this vast area in the Wei river valley, about 227,000 hectares, supported extra soldiers and the strategic advantage of the canal was much improved communications. In short, the Chengkuo canal turned Qin into the chief economic area, a place where agricultural productivity and facilities for transport permitted a supply of tax-grain so superior to other places, that the ruler who controlled it could control all China.

In the account of the canal's construction it is interesting that the Han king assumed the willingness of Qin to adopt public works on a scale greater than any other state. This reputation for innovation must have been a legacy of Shang Yang's ministry, which lasted from 356 till 338 B.C. Yet it should not be overlooked that the project was so extensive that even the Qin king hesitated on hearing about the plot, though he was persuaded to continue by the engineer, who may have only realised himself during the course of the work what it would mean for Qin once it had been completed. Another version of the interview has Cheng Kuo saying: "I have, by this ruse, prolonged the life of the state of Han for a few years, but I am accomplishing a scheme which will sustain Qin for ten thousand generations."

Since learning hardly existed in backward Qin, its rulers were forced to look beyond their borders for talented people to employ. Like Cheng Kuo, the statesman Yang Shang had earlier travelled westwards to try his fortune. Gaining the ear of the Qin ruler, he thoroughly reformed the state by means of a new law code aimed at increasing military strength. Following the precepts of the School of Law (which Han Fei Zi was to lead), Shang Yang sought to weaken the aristocracy, break up powerful clans, and free the peasants from bondage; in place of customary ties he substituted collective responsibility as a method of securing order. The implementation of such fundamental measures was by no means easy, though dissention did not long outlast the shaming of the heir to the throne. When the crown prince transgressed one of the new laws, Shang Yang demanded that at least there should be a token punishment. The king therefore agreed that the prince's guardian be degraded and the face of the prince's tutor tattooed, presumably on the grounds that these nobles shared responsibility for the prince's misbehaviour.

Such fanaticism cost Shang Yang dear. Unloved, and feared by the nobles and the common people alike, the minister was safe as long as his patron remained on the throne, but once the disgraced prince succeeded in 338 B.C., Shang Yang's enemies swiftly accused him of sedition and officers were sent to arrest him. There is marvellous justice in the story of his attempted flight. The ex-minister at first tried to hide in an obscure inn, but the inn-keeper, in ignorance of his identity, told him that under the new laws he dared not admit a man without a permit for fear of punishment. So it was that Shang Yang personally learned of the thoroughness of his own law code.

Realising that escape from Qin was equally impossible because of his renown, he returned to his country estate and prepared to resist. Defeat and dishonour were his fate, for as an example to the rebellious, the corpse of Shang Yang was torn limb from limb by chariots and all the members of his family were exterminated.

Whilst Sima Qian felt that "the bad end Shang Yang came to in Qin was no more than he deserved," he is an honest enough historian to record the amazing effect of the minister's reforms. He noted that

by the end of ten years the Qin people were acquiescent. Nothing lost on the road was picked up and pocketed, the hills were free of bandits, every household prospered, men fought bravely on the battlefield but avoided quarrels at home, and good government existed in both towns and villages.

*Unarmoured
warrior.*

On Qin, Shang Yang had imposed Legalism, the most severe philosophy of the so-called Warring States period (481-221 B.C.). Its basic idea was the standardisation of society as a means of increasing the power of the ruler. Obedience to the letter of the law was demanded. As we have already noticed, Han Fei Zi soon was to term compassion as one of the Five Lice. It was not unexpected then, that once the First Emperor held undisputed sway over the Chinese people, the harsh doctrines of Legalism should involve the burning of books containing different points of view and the execution of philosophical opponents. The great rebellion that overthrew the Qin dynasty in 206 B.C. can in fact be regarded as a rising of China against this bullying law code.

Other philosophies competed for supremacy during the turbulent centuries preceding the foundation of the Chinese empire in 221 B.C. The main schools of thought besides Legalism, were Confucianism, Daoism and Moism. Although the pacific doctrines of the latter closely challenged those of the School of Law, both of these philosophies were to decline after the fall of the Qin dynasty. It has been said that traditionally the Chinese were always Daoist in private and Confucianist in public, but a scholar living in the First Emperor's reign would have been pessimistic about the survival of the teachings of both Confucius and Lao Zi.

The moral philosophy of Confucius (551-479 B.C.), with its emphasis on family obligations and learning, seemed almost irrelevant when confronted by Qin indifference to ordinary feelings. For neither scholarship nor ritual had a recognised place in an empire dedicated to the will of an absolute ruler. Only under the succeeding dynasty, the Han, were the Confucian virtues of service and loyalty to come into their own as the yardsticks of behaviour for the imperial civil servant.

Despite Zheng's fascination for magic, the fortunes of Daoism were no less bleak: they were even more threatened whenever Daoist magicians had to report the continued absence of the elixir of life. Lao Zi (born 604 B.C.), the legendary founder of Daoism, would have found the First Emperor's manic desire for control quite pointless, since he took the view that wisdom was so hard to find because of the artificial demands made on mankind by society. As his greatest follower Zhuang Zi (350-275 B.C.) cynically remarked: "A thief steals a purse and is hanged, while another man steals a state and becomes a king."

Such a sentiment did not give Zheng reason to pause though, once he became First Emperor. He gave full scope to the Legalist policies of his Grand Councillor, Li Si, who reminded him of the dangers in assigning feudal territories to his relations. Li Si commented:

"The Zhou kings gave lands to their sons, younger brothers and many other members of their clans, but later descendants fell out and finally set on each other. And when their states engaged in war, the king of Zhou was powerless to stop them. Now thanks to Your Majesty's divine might, all the land within the Four Seas has become your provinces. If you give the princes and men who have served you well official salaries and money rewards, they will be easy to control and there will be no strife in the empire. This is the way to peace, not the re-establishment of feudal lords!"

So feudal holdings were abolished and noble families compelled to take up residence in Xianyang, now the capital of all China. At least 120,000 families were moved in 221 B.C. alone. Next imperial edicts gave the peasantry greater rights over their land but made them liable for taxes and labour on public works; divided the empire into new administrative districts with garrisons planted at strategic points; set up a body of inspectors to oversee the administration of justice and tax collection; standardised weights and measures, currency, axle wheels and the written language; constructed a national network of roads and canals; and to counter threats from the northern nomads, built the Great Wall.

帝 皇 始 秦

An old drawing of Qin Shi Huangdi, which captures something of the anxiety he undoubtedly suffered.

The pace was phenomenal. By 213 B.C. the murmurings against these changes were even heard at court, and so Li Si suggested outright repression of the critics, especially Confucian scholars. The Grand Councillor said:

"In the past the empire was disunited. Because there was no emperor, the feudal lords were active and in order to confuse the people they harped on antiquity . . . . Now Your Majesty rules a unified empire in which distinctions of right and wrong are as clear as your own unapproachable authority. Yet there are those who unofficially propagate teachings directed against imperial decrees and orders. When they hear new instructions, they criticize them in the light of their own teachings. At court they only dare to disagree in their minds, but in the streets they openly criticize your commands. To cast disrepute on their ruler they look upon as a duty; to adhere to contrary views they consider a virtue. The people are thus encouraged to be disrespectful. If this slander is not stopped, the imperial authority will decline and factionalism ensue . . . .

"Your servant requests that all persons possessing works of literature . . . and discussions of philosophers should destroy them. Those who have not destroyed them within thirty days after the issuing of the order are to be branded and sent to work as convicts. Books to be spared from destruction will be those on medicine,

agriculture, and divination. As for persons who wish to study, let them take the officials as their teachers."

The First Emperor approved Li Si's recommendation and the book burning took place to "make the people ignorant" and to prevent "the use of the past to discredit the present." The exemption of works on divination may have been calculated, given Zheng's interest in the spirit world, but the minister may have recognised that the deeply rooted and widespread belief in its efficacy would make suppression very difficult. Sweeping though Li Si's measure was in its attempt to make knowledge an imperial monopoly, the destruction of books under Qin rulers was not new; Shang Yang had already in the fourth century B.C. burned the Histories.

The ultimate result was decisive, nonetheless. When in 206 B.C. a rebel army sacked Xianyang, the flames engulfed the imperial library and in many cases destroyed the sole remaining copies. The loss caused a definite break in consciousness, for when under the patronage of the Han emperors ancient texts were painfully reconstructed, the world of the feudal states prior to 221 B.C. seemed remote.

The Qin unification of China as an empire was a political fact. Although the dynasty lasted for only fifteen years, such was the energy and determination of its founder that the period represents a turning point in Chinese history, for the bureaucratic form of government developed under the Qin emperors became the model for future political organisation in China, lasting until our own century. The historical significance of the sweeping alteration the First Emperor began and Liu Bang was to complete cannot be underestimated. They showed the Chinese people the value of unity. Since 221 B.C. the country has been united for a longer period than it has been disunited, thus making China an exception to the rule that in the pre-modern era large states do not endure.

An armoured infantryman in Pit No. 1.

Detail of his boo armour, showin the rivets used t hold the iron pl together. (right)

THE CHINESE ART OF WAR

That one of the greatest achievements of the Chinese empire was to be the triumph of civil over military culture hardly a person who lived through the reign of the First Emperor could have believed. Yet this humane approach to conflict, and its place in organised society, is a trait that has consistently marked China out from other countries.

A reluctance to glorify war found its justification in the idea that the superior man should be able to attain his ends without violence. Fundamental to the teachings of Confucius, whose philosophy was adopted in the first century B.C. as the official orthodoxy, this rejection of coercion always meant that it was never easy to glorify war because ideally it should never have occurred. Morality always inclined towards peace and the pressing need to ensure its maintenance. So deep went this attitude that during the crisis of the early empire, known as the Three Kingdoms (221-265), the Chinese derived from a contemporary general their god of war, Guan Di. Where he differs from other deities is in his pacific intentions, for Guan Di was neither bloodthirsty like the Greek Ares nor an implacable foe like the Roman Mars; on the contrary, he was a power dedicated to the prevention of conflict.

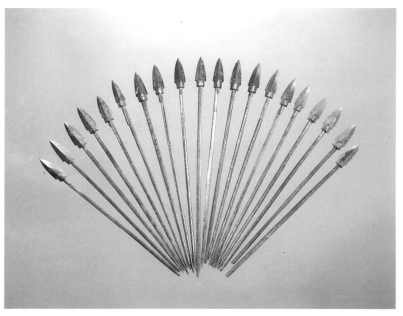

Bronze crossbow bolts.

Possibily the comparative isolation of ancient China from other centres of civilisation helped to keep the military in their place. While foreign conquest and warfare in Rome became a major industry, China consistently adopted a defensive stance and saw in the Great Wall the best means of dealing with the nomad menace that troubled the northern provinces from the fall of Hao in 771 B.C. onwards. When it is recalled that the Chinese also invented the crossbow (before 450 B.C.) and the gun (in the twelfth century), this disavowal of military adventure appears even more amazing.

Some of the credit for this must be given to the First Emperor himself. Because he was one of the great destroyers of history, the ruthless regime which his officials sought to impose on the Chinese people fully exposed the narrowness of the military mind. The inevitable reaction was the first national rebellion ever recorded in China, which in 206 B.C. swept away the Qin dynasty and only left behind the terracotta army as testimony of its once awesome power.

Reconstruction of a Qin crossbow.

Close-ups of the armour worn by a kneeling crossbowman.

The life-sized warriors in the underground chambers at Mount Li can indeed be seen as a memorial to all the men who fell in the unusual violence of the centuries down to 221 B.C. Their armour and weapons leave no doubt as to the ferocity of the battles in which they fought. The Histories provide an outline of the ever growing scale of conflict, but we are able to interpret individual wars with a degree of certainty because of the survival of Sun Zi's *Art of War* (*Zhanshu*), the oldest military treatise in the world. Dating probably from the early fourth century B.C., this document explains the strategy best followed by generals on campaign. It is divided into thirteen sections, covering topics such as planning, waging war, offensive action, tactical dispositions, energy, weak and strong points, manoeuvring, variations of tactics, marches, terrain, varieties of ground, attack by fire, and the use of spies. The opening lines tell us that "war is of vital importance to the state; a matter of life or death; a road either to survival or ruin. That is why its study cannot be neglected."

The hangar-like roof built over Pit No. 1.

Although Sun Zi discusses the detail of war, he believes that the moral strength and intellectual faculty of man is critical in securing a victory or avoiding a defeat. No military adventure should be undertaken thoughtlessly or recklessly, since preliminary moves are an essential part of strategy. The plans of an enemy can be countered in advance, mistrust spread among his allies, and the morale of his forces weakened to the point where the will to fight is lost. Only when the enemy cannot be overcome by any other method than a direct attack, should a commander offer battle, and then the fighting needs to be swift and economical of human life. As great generals have always understood, the chief target in any conflict is the mind of the opposing commander. When this has been probed, there ought to be no difficulty in recognising the opportune moment to strike.

Strictness of discipline ensured that the order of attack would be properly followed. How severe military regulation should be in a model army is shown in a story that Sun Zi quotes with approval. He writes:

Gongs and drums, banners and flags are used to hold the attention of the troops. When the troops can be thus united, the brave cannot advance alone, nor can the cowardly fall back. This is known as the art of deploying a host. Therefore, those who when they should advance do not do so and those who when they should retire do not do so are beheaded.

When, for instance, Chu fought against Qin there was an officer who before the battle was unable to control himself. He advanced and took a pair of heads and returned. The Chu general ordered his execution. When it was pointed out how brave and talented the officer was, the general said: "I am sure that he is an officer of ability, but he is disobedient." So he beheaded him at once.

Yet it was in fact the state of Qin which first broke the power of the hereditary aristocracy in the army by promoting after 350 B.C. only the brave and the obedient.

*Corridors of troops
in the same
underground
chamber.*

Prior to the reforms of Shang Yang the forces of Qin had come to battle like any other army. In spite of a reputation for taking the offensive, Qin armies tolerated the archery duels that their nobleman delighted to conduct with the enemy before the fight commenced. These mannered skirmishes were the Chinese equivalent of chivalry and, daring though many of the chariot raids must have been, they did not contribute very much to the outcome of the general engagement. The death sentence passed upon the Chu officer for his revival of this personal duelling is evidence of the change in tactics that followed the invention of the crossbow.

Cavalry mount

The abandonment of the chariot as the main arm of war in the face of deadly shafts dispatched by crossbowmen during the fifth century B.C. ended aristocratic domination of the battlefield. Although the advice of ancestral spirits might still be sought before the decision to fight was reached, there was never any question that everything hinged on the performance of the footsoldier. Battles had turned into large-scale infantry contests, massed armoured columns supported by crossbowmen, cavalry and chariots. There was less ritual and more organised slaughter as hundreds of thousands of infantrymen crashed into each other. Not until the iron stirrup appeared in China shortly before the Three Kingdoms period and turned horseriders into real cavalry, was there a challenge to the importance of infantry.

The chariot had never been a very efficient fighting machine, however. While it acted as a mobile platform for archers and spearmen, the ground over which a chariot could run tended to be limited to the plains of the major river valleys. As early as 541 B.C. a Jin general had abandoned chariots and reorganised his soldiers into infantry squads in order to deal with barbarians along the mountainous northern frontier. The king of Zhao, who inherited the same military problem during the Warring States period, in 307 B.C. went so far as to adopt the barbarian fashion of wearing trousers, for his newly formed cavalry. This imitation of nomad horse tactics proved useful on the borders of the steppe, where speed was needed to rush troops to points threatened by sudden raids, but it did little to influence either the armoured masses of infantry or those lethal auxiliaries, the crossbowmen, whose weapon outranged all others in the battles fought down to 221 B.C.

In the final two centuries prior to the unification of China that year war was not just professional and serious, it was also expensive as larger states absorbed smaller neighbours and

Cavalryman with mount. Qin horses, according to the Histories, 'could jump twelve paces.'

ploughed more resources into the military field. The powerful states of Qin and Chu could each mobilise over 1 million soldiers. Since the core of armies were regulars, highly trained and well equipped officers and men, rulers were anxious to protect what was a considerable investment. As Sun Zi remarks:

In operations of war, where there are in the field a thousand fast chariots, as many heavy chariots, and a hundred thousand armoured infantrymen, with provisions to carry the host a distance of a thousand li, the expenditure at home and at the front, including the cost of sundry items and entertainment, will amount to one thousand pieces of gold a day. Only when this money is in hand, should a force of this size be raised. Because when an army marches abroad, the treasury will be emptied at home. For this reason a long campaign or a seige will not only blunt the weapons of the soldiers and depress their morale, it will also exhaust the resources of the state. Now, when your weapons are dulled, your ardour damped, your strength exhausted and your treasure spent, other rulers will swiftly take advantage of your distress. Then no adviser, however wise, will be able to avert the consequences that must ensue.

Qin coin, the standard of the Chinese empire.

Armies were simply war-machines with no scope for noble display. The cost of their maintenance in time of peace could be offset by the labour duties which the regulars performed, as members of the People's Liberation Army continue to do in China today. Besides cultivating land, professional soldiers were expected to assist with irrigation schemes and road building. In 212 B.C. we know that the Qin general Meng Tian set 300,000 troops to work on the construction of the Great Wall and its approach road from Xianyang, after clearing the Ordos desert of nomad raiders. But as soon as hostilities had started, the full expense of "one thousand pieces of gold a day," or more, fell on the state treasury. Hence, the tremendous advantage of Zheng in planning his campaigns, once the increased agricultural wealth produced by the Chengkuo canal flowed into his coffers. Unlike other kings, he could afford to keep his army on campaign throughout the growing season. War for Qin did not depend upon raiding enemy supplies to supplement its own food stocks – "foraging on the enemy" is one of the economy measures Sun Zi recommends – because improved harvests in the Wei river valley already provided a handsome surplus that could be stored against military needs. A tactical benefit for its expeditionary forces, living entirely on waggons filled with home-grown grain, was a freedom of maneouvre denied to opponents.

Alongside the new professionalism there emerged a ruthlessness that would have stunned Sun Zi, whose entire concern in the *Art of War* is the limitation of casualties. To the horror of the Chinese people, Qin generals turned the ceremonial execution of a handful of prisoners after a fight into massacre. At Chang Ping in 260 B.C., the Histories say, the blood of 400,000 Zhao prisoners was "shed for the drums." Allowing for anti-Qin exaggeration on the part of later writers, it is still apparent that the Qin army inflicted a staggering number of casualties upon opposing forces. From the records of battles we possess the combined total of enemy

Looking across
No. 1.
(right)

Cavalryman.

soldiers it killed in action from Shang Yang's ministry till the enthronement of the First Emperor amounts to just under 1.5 million. Even this casuality list is incomplete, because the wounded are excluded as well as enemy losses sustained in the campaigns for which no figures are given.

An acceleration of conflict following the accession of Zheng to the Qin throne can be deduced from the Histories. The sequence of campaigns is impressive.

233 B.C.   Li Si urges the Qin king to conquer Han in order to intimidate all the feudal states.

232 B.C.   Qin generals, including Wang Jian, invade Han and capture nine cities.

230 B.C.   The state of Han is destroyed. Qin forces also enter Zhao and defeat its army at the battle of Ping Yang, killing 100,000 men.

229 B.C.   Further Qin attacks are directed against the state of Zhao.

228 B.C.   A great force crosses the Yellow river from Qin and destroys Zhao.

227 B.C.   In reaction to the attempt on his life by Jing Ke, Zheng orders increased military activity.

226 B.C.   Attacks are launched against Wei, Qi and Chu, although the latter campaign ends in a serious reverse.

225 B.C.   The state of Wei is annexed to Qin.

223 B.C.   The veteran Wang Jian succeeds to redeeming Qin prestige by his conquest of Chu.

222 B.C.   A great force is sent against Yan, which falls after a fierce campaign.

221 B.C.   Qi, once the state of hegemon Huan, surrenders to Qin, 'master of all the land.'

*Figures from Pit
No. 2.*

Of these campaigns the most critical was Wang Jian's invasion of Chu, the only state that could have defeated Qin. Because Zheng was so worried about its conduct, and accompanied the army on the initial march, a look at the strategy employed by the veteran should be instructive.

The defeat suffered by Qin in 226 B.C. had resulted from Zheng's misjudgment of the strength of Chu. He had decided to entrust the attack to a comparatively inexperienced commander, for no other reason than that he offered to accomplish the task with 200,000 troops, one-third of the number which Wang Jian said were required. The mauling suffered by the expeditionary force compelled the strong-willed king to beg the old soldier for help. 'You are not too old', Zheng insisted, 'and you can lead the army. Grant my request, for my kingdom is in disorder, and this great defeat must be avenged by a crowning victory over Chu.'

Wang Jian agreed to come out of retirement on condition that the size of his army should be 600,000 men. The news that Wang Jian was to command the Qin invasion force quickly brought enough men to the colours to reach this total. Accompanied by Zheng, the wily general set off for the border of Chu in 223 B.C. On the journey southwards, however, Wang Jian asked for gifts of land and property, which were readily granted. 'Only defeat the enemy', said king Zheng, 'and you will never need to reproach me for my generosity.' But Wang Jian replied:

'If it pleases Your Majesty, I would rather have gifts now. Your way of bestowing rewards is different from other dynasties. You reward men with high office which ceases with their death. Other rulers bestow titles and lands that they pass on to their children. My office dies with me, and so I ask for these lands and houses that I may give them to my children in the event of my death in the present campaign.'

A detachment of armoured infantrymen.

Armoured warrior.

Zheng constantly sought to reassure Wang Jian, even sending letters to him once he had crossed into enemy territory. By making the requests, the commander informed his officers, he hoped to maintain the king's confidence. 'In the gifts,' Wang Jian said, 'he has a guarantee of my loyalty. By rebellion I would risk them all, and by treason I could not gain more.'

The apprehensiveness of Wang Jian was probably justified. In the emergency he commanded a powerful army and he enjoyed unlimited authority. At court there would have been those who plotted against him, insinuating that his conduct of the war cloaked greater ambitions. Moreover, he knew that he could not chance a hasty engagement with the enemy. The bravery of Chu soldiers was legion and in defending their homes they would offer the most determined resistance on the battlefield. As his own reputation as a commander was well known, it was to be expected that every effort would be made to assemble a mighty army. Already his spies informed him that volunteers from every part of Chu were flocking to enlist, while regular units were securing strongholds in order to slow his own advance.

"All warfare," Sun Zi notes, "is based on deception. Therefore, when capable, pretend incapability; when active, inactivity. Above all else, pretend inferiority and encourage the arrogance of the enemy commander." Thus Wang Jian proceeded by cunning strategy to unbalance the numerous defenders. He entrenched his army in a strongly fortified camp, and there he behaved as though his soldiers had not come for the serious purpose of war, but for a prolonged holiday. They swam, sang and feasted. In the meantime the Chu army began to look with contempt upon the invaders. Had they not turned back one Qin army already? Were not the troops of Wang Jian unwilling to risk a second defeat? The Chu soldiers relaxed, loosened their discipline, and lost their alertness. As soon as Wang Jian perceived the moment to

strike had arrived, he sent his forces crashing into the ill-prepared Chu army and secured an overwhelming victory. According to the Histories:

the Chu king was taken prisoner, the commander-in-chief slain, and the whole army scattered, never to be assembled again as a fighting force. The state itself was immediately annexed to Qin, and so became part of the already extensive domain of Zheng.

Wang Jian had sallied forth when he was sure that the Chu army was off guard: by delivering the knock-out blow when they was least able to resist, the enemy were put to flight at little cost to his own forces.

As the *Art of War* recognises, 'those skilled in war avoid the enemy when his spirit is keen and attack him when it is sluggish and his soldiers homesick. This control is called the moral factor.' The collapse of Chu after this victory assured the triumph of Qin and the unification of China. The campaigns of 222 and 221 B.C. were the last in the series of attacks on the feudal states initiated by Zheng – though Yan put up a stout fight, after 223 B.C. there was no state capable of stopping the "Tiger of Qin."

Unarmoured
warrior. His clothes
were probably
cotton.

Having eliminated his last earthly rival to absolute power in 221 B.C., Zheng turned his attention to securing the position which he proposed to occupy in the after-life. While Li Si pressed on with the reorganisation of China within a unified empire, the First Emperor simultaneously sought the elixir of life from the Immortals and directed the construction of his own mausoleum at Mount Li, some forty kilometres east of Xianyang. The defence of his tomb was placed in the hands of two distinct forces: the soldiers who guarded the site above ground from human marauders, and the terracotta warriors who were to deal with spirit enemies below. That the preparations for subterranean defence were so carefully laid shows how uncertain the First Emperor was in his own mind about what might await him after death. Quite possibly Zheng imagined that his old enemies would wreck their vengeance upon him then, because he deliberately stationed the terracotta army to the east of his grave – the direction from which they would have approached.

Today the tumulus at Mount Li looks rather like a low hill. Sited midway between a mountain and the Wei river, its disposition obviously conforms to ancient Daoist practices of geomancy that attempted to ensure the harmony of the deceased. Other than the tumulus itself, the material remains of the mausoleum complex have largely vanished above ground, although there are traces of several rammed-earth walls belonging to an enclosure. But excavation has revealed that the two main walls were aligned to the pole star, a constellation with which the ruler was compared in China from earliest times. "He who exercises government by means of his virtue," Confucius said, "may be likened to the pole star, which keeps its place while all the others turn around it." The Son of Heaven was expected to dwell, according to geomantic tradition, at "the place where earth and sky meet, where the four seasons merge, where wind and rain are gathered in, and where the elements are in harmony." Just as the influence of

*Crossbowman from
the vanguard of Pit
No. 1.*

54

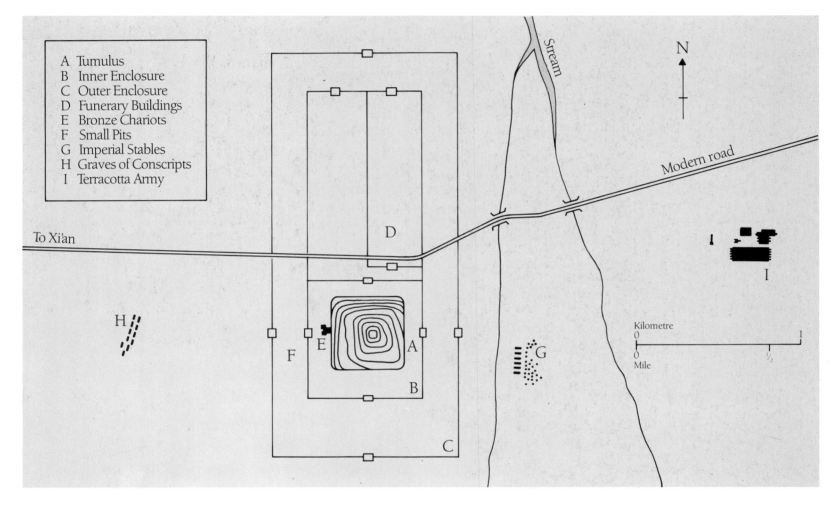

A Tumulus
B Inner Enclosure
C Outer Enclosure
D Funerary Buildings
E Bronze Chariots
F Small Pits
G Imperial Stables
H Graves of Conscripts
I Terracotta Army

To Xi'an

Stream

Modern road

N

D

H

F E A

B

C

G

Kilometre
0   1
0   ½
Mile

I

Mount Li showing the First Emperor's tomb.

Plan of Pit No.1. The Infantry Regiment.   o o o Unarmoured soldiers.   ● ● ● Armoured soldiers.   [⊞] Six chariots containing officers.

the ruler on earth radiated in all directions, so the hours were thought to radiate from the pole. In the north-south orientation of Beijing, the final imperial capital, the same cosmological pattern can still be seen to persist. In 1421 the Ming emperor Yong Le ordered this city to be built within a city wall in such a way that all the terraces and openings of principal buildings faced south.

The two walls surrounding the First Emperor's grave measure 2,173 by 974 metres and 685 by 578 metres respectively; the total area once enclosed was nearly two square kilometres. Both of these walls were each pierced by four gates, while to the north of the tumulus another wall subdivided the inner enclosure. A number of funerary buildings unearthed here in 1977 may have served as a

"sleeping palace," a dormitory for the worshippers attending ceremonies within the sacred precinct. From records of later imperial burial customs we are aware that high-born worshippers regularly visited an emperor's tomb in order to make sacrifices. In addition to commissioning a new capital at Beijing, Yong Le prepared an imperial necropolis for the Ming dynasty in an auspicious valley amid a range of hills fifty kilometres to the north. We know how he entrusted the protection of the cemetery to a permanent garrison of soldiers, which patrolled the outer ramparts and guarded each tomb as soon as it was built; and how within the necropolis, he settled guardian families (*linfu*), charging them with its general maintenance as well as the supply of the ingredients used for the cycle of sacrifices. But Yong Le did not attempt to indulge in the extravagance of a life-sized terracotta army.

Looking eastwards
in Pit No. 1.

The placing of pottery figures in the vaults of tombs was a popular practice in ancient China – indeed the display cases of modern museums are now filled with their fascinating variety of forms – but no other ruler seems to have tried to compete with the scale of the First Emperor's preparations for the after-life. Yet we should not overlook the fact that Zheng never used his personal eminence to reverse the trend against human sacrifice, even though it was a consequence of the Confucian teaching he so detested. In 384 B.C. Qin had outlawed this barbaric custom, thereby following the lead of the more advanced feudal states. Although a number of people were put to death on the First Emperor's internment, their execution seems to have been the responsibility of his successor. In the Histories we read:

As soon as the First Emperor became king of Qin [in 246 B.C.] work was begun on his mausoleum at Mount Li. After he won the empire [in 221 B.C.], more than 700,000 conscripts from all parts of China laboured there. They dug through three underground streams; they poured molten copper for the outer coffin; and they filled the burial chamber with models of palaces, towers and official buildings, as well as fine utensils, precious stones and rarities. Artisans were ordered to fix automatic crossbows so that grave robbers would be slain. The waterways of the empire, the Yellow and Yangzi rivers, and even the great ocean itself, were represented by mercury and were made to flow mechanically. Above, the heavenly constellations were depicted, while below lay a representation of the earth. Lamps using whale oil were installed to burn for a long time.

The Second Emperor decreed [in 210 B.C.] that his father's childless concubines should follow him to the grave. After they were duly buried an official suggested that the artisans responsible for the mechanical devices knew too much about the contents of the tomb for safety. Therefore, once the First Emperor was placed in the burial chamber and the treasures were sealed up, the middle and outer gates were shut to imprison all those who had worked on the tomb. No one came out.

Although the unusual size of the tumulus (1,400 metres in circumference and 43 metres in height) corresponds with this description of the burial, the remainder of the mausoleum site gives no immediate suggestion of the other splendours hidden underground. Nothing in the historical record or local folk lore can be said to refer to the terracotta army either. A couple of large kneeling figures in terracotta had been unearthed close to the tumulus before its discovery in 1974, but they were found close to the surface of the ground and in no discernable order. The terracotta army, on the contrary, was deployed in military fashion within specially constructed subterranean chambers.

The first one to be discovered, Pit No. 1, is rectangular in shape and measures 210 by 60 metres. This chamber was skilfully built: the rammed earth surrounding the corridors and galleries prevented subsidence, while the chamber was paved with bricks and its wooden roof was supported by stout timber pillars and crossbeams. To prevent moisture seeping down from the surface, the roof was covered by woven matting and then a layer of clay. It is likely that the rebel soldiers were able to find the pits containing the terracotta army in 206 B.C. because the soil excavated from them rose in small tell-tale mounds.

Running from east to west, Pit No. 1 is divided into eleven parallel corridors, nine measuring 3 metres in width and two measuring just under 2 metres. At the east and west ends, a gallery runs from north to south, with five earthern ramps leading to the surface. Of the estimated 6,000 terracotta warriors in Pit No. 1, the majority are armoured infantrymen whose officers ride in six chariots almost at the front of the

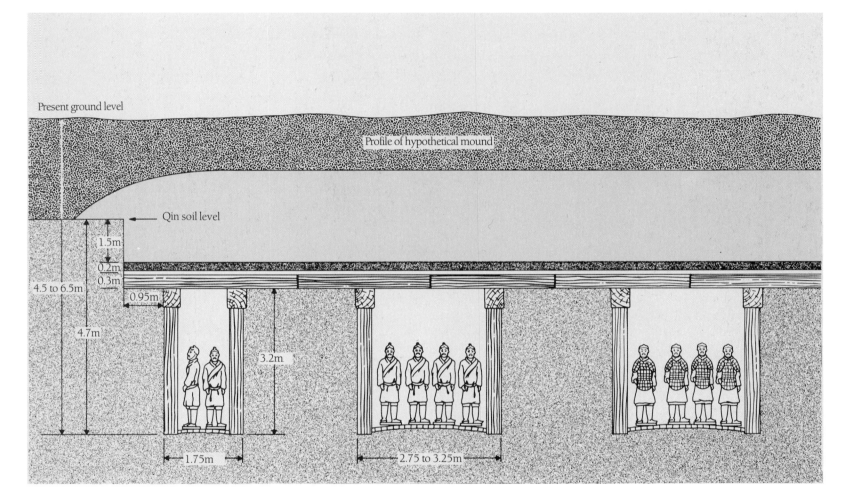

Present ground level

Profile of hypothetical mound

Qin soil level

1.5m

0.2m
0.3m

4.5 to 6.5m

4.7m

0.95m

3.2m

1.75m

2.75 to 3.25m

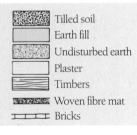 Tilled soil

Earth fill

Undisturbed earth

Plaster

Timbers

Woven fibre mat

Bricks

Cross-section of Pit
No. 1.

formation. These footsoldiers do not wear helmets, but their armour offers protection to the upper part of the body as well as the shoulders.

Seven types of armour have been found amongst the terracotta army. The Histories tell us that during the Warring States period both iron-mail coats and iron weapons existed, although so far few examples of coats of mail have survived. The numerous iron slates used in their design were joined so that the top pieces pressed down on the ones below. It is thought that a mail coat was put on and taken off over the head, the button for fastening it tight being on the upper right side, where the coat opens and closes. Because the iron would have rubbed against the necks of the soldiers and caused sores, each man is also shown wearing a protective scarf. Today the overall appearance of the restored warriors in Pit No. 1 is greyish brown. Once there were probably two colour schemes for the armoured infantrymen: one group had black slates with white rivets, gold buttons, and purple cords, their tunics being green, their trousers dark blue, and their shoes black with red laces; a second group wore brown slated armour with red rivets and orange buttons and cords, the rest of their uniform being the same as the first group, except that their shorter tunics were red.

The heads of all the warriors were painted as well: the eyes were white with black irises, while the eyebrows, whiskers and hair were black. The painting of statutary was common throughout the Old World – our modern view of the plainness of ancient sculpture having been caused by the ravages of time – but there can be no question of how impressive the multi-coloured infantry unit in Pit No. 1 originally must have been.

In the vanguard, standing just before the officers in the chariots, are three rows each of 68 unarmoured men. Dressed

Kneeling crossbowman.

60

*Unarmoured Qin
soldier.*

in light cotton clothes in order to assist fast movement, these crossbowmen delivered with their bolts the punch that disrupted the enemy ranks prior to a Qin charge. According to the Histories, Qin infantrymen were renowned for their bravery. They did not only disdain to wear helmets. It is recorded how they abandonned their clumsy coats of mail on entering the fray so as to move easily and strike down the enemy with their halberds and swords. The powerful weapon that prepared for this onslaught was the crossbow, which came into general use from the early fourth century B.C. onwards. Bows reconstructed from the fragmentary remains and impressions found in the pits at Mount Li are approximately 71 cm in length, with a groove at the front in which the bolt rested and a bronze trigger mechanism at the rear. The range and destructiveness of these crossbows were greater than any other weapon then in existence. Had the First Emperor's army chanced to encounter either Macedonian or Roman troops, the discharge of its crossbows would have made colanders of their shields.

Although the crossbow is supposed to have been used by some of William the Conqueror's forces at Hastings in 1066, the advent of this weapon on the battlefields of Europe seems to have occurred somewhat after that date. However, the papacy soon recognised the new dimension that it brought to war, the Lateran Council of 1139 declaring the crossbow too murderous for use against fellow Christians. As in China, it was found to be an excellent weapon for defensive shooting, particularly from a concealed position on a high wall.

Apart from mention of crossbowmen along the Great Wall and the archaeological evidence afforded by the deployment of the terracotta army's vanguard, we lack information concerning the role of the crossbow in the campaigns Zheng directed. The nearest recorded engagement in which its power was clearly demonstrated took place in 99 B.C. well beyond the line of the Great Wall. Operating against the Huns,

the Han general Li Ling was the first Chinese to engage the nomad horsemen on foot. Denied cavalry support through a misunderstanding at court, Li Ling's force of 5,000 infantry was surrounded by 30,000 enemy horsemen and his line of retreat blocked. So he drew his men up, ordering the front ranks to bear halberbs and shields. Behind these armoured footsoldiers stood a thousand crossbowmen, whose task it was to fire upon the outranged nomad archers as soon as they could be sure of inflicting casualties. The effect was appalling and the Huns were forced to withdraw. Had Li Ling's supply of bolts been greater, or Chinese reinforcements arrived to exploit his victory, the battle would have gone down in history as a decisive one for tactical innovation. As it was, the Hunnish leader heard of his shortage of ammunition from a traitor and renewed the attack until the Chinese soldiers were obliged to flee. What Li Ling almost demonstrated was that infantry, when properly organised and supplied with enough crossbows, could vanquish an overwhelming force of mounted archers.

Other weapons carried by the terracotta army were the sword and the halberd, a combination of spear and battleaxe. The group of unarmoured warriors at the front of the central corridor of Pit No. 1 were almost certainly armed with the latter, as were one of the officers in each of the chariots. A blow from the protruding edge of a halberd would have knocked an opponent to his knees in the tumult of hand-to-hand fighting. If swung from a moving chariot, an extended halberd could have hardly missed even a distant target. The head of this weapon was made from bronze, just like the sword recovered from Pit No. 1 in 1981. There is in fact no basis for the theory that the triumph of Qin over the other feudal states was due to its development of low-grade steel weapons. From the archaeological testimony the soldiers of Qin seem to have favoured bronze weapons whose extra sharpness resulted from a chromium coating.

比例: 1/4

比例: 1/4

比例: 1/5

比例: 1/4

比例: 1/4

比例: 1/4

*Part of supposed
colour scheme of the
terracotta army.*

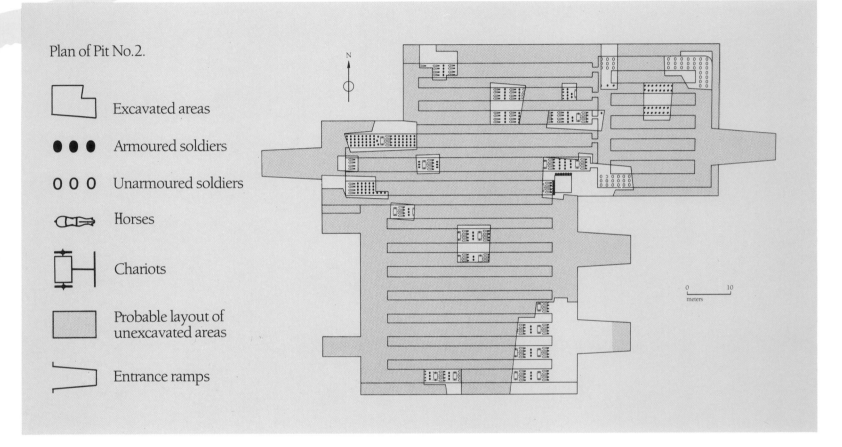

Plan of Pit No.2.

Excavated areas

● ● ● Armoured soldiers

O O O Unarmoured soldiers

Horses

Chariots

Probable layout of unexcavated areas

Entrance ramps

N

0   10
meters

A second underground chamber, Pit No. 2, was found in 1976 and partially excavated. Situated slightly to the north of Pit No. 1, its fourteen parallel corridors held a mixed force deployed in a curved formation. The first of the four detachments unearthed here, at the very front of the curve, consists of 334 crossbowmen in standing and kneeling positions. Close by a general is stationed, along with a small staff of officers. The second detachment in the formation is a block of 64 chariots standing at the tail end of the curve. There are eight rows of eight chariots, each vehicle manned by a driver and two guards. No footsoldiers are found in this section of Pit No. 2 at all. The third detachment, in the centre

of the curve, includes 19 chariots, 264 armoured infantry and eight cavalry, standing in three columns. Unlike the block of chariots, the footsoldiers are intended to fight alongside the chariots as a mixed skirmishing unit. The final detachment is almost entirely cavalry, 108 horsemen and six chariots.

From Pit No. 2 comes the kneeling crossbowmen so admired in exhibitions of the terracotta army outside China. The incredible detail of this figure extends to the condition of his footware, with a clear impression of the grip on the soles of his boots. Traces of pigment suggest that he wore a blue tunic and trousers, while his cuffs, scarf and hair ribbon were red.

Crossbowman from
Pit No. 2, and the
sole of his boot.

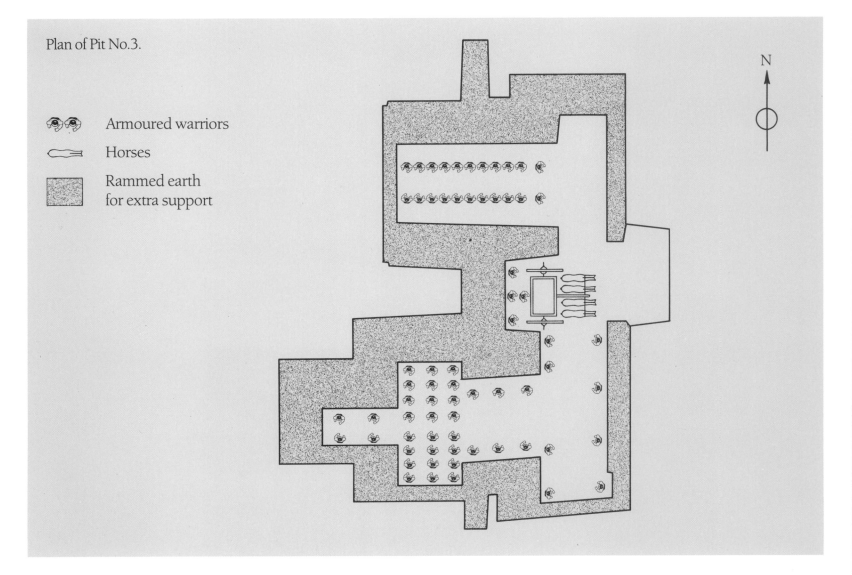

Plan of Pit No.3.

Armoured warriors

Horses

Rammed earth
for extra support

N

The final part of the terracotta army was buried in Pit No. 3, the only chamber to be fully explored. It is irregular in shape and small, about one-seventh of the area of Pit No. 1. Untouched by the rebels in 206 B.C., Pit No. 3 appears to have been the command post of the commander-in-chief, although this particular figure is missing. An empty fourth pit indicates that the terracotta army was incomplete on the fall of the Qin dynasty and so we may never gaze upon the face of the man who once commanded the First Emperor's personal guard. But the remains of his war chariot are there; its unusual feature was a roof or canopy, presumably to give protection from the elements.

The toggle at the
top right allowed
Qin soldiers to
throw off their
armour when they
entered the fray.

The padded
trousers and boots
worn by the
terracotta army.

Despite the staggering number of life-sized figures in the ranks of the terracotta army, warriors and horses were not stamped from moulds, but individually modelled. Great pains were taken to build up each piece from the course grey clay found in the vicinity of Mount Li. Its plastic qualities must have assisted the potter-sculptors as they fashioned each hollow torso above its solid legs, and then added the finishing touches on the surface in a finer clay. The smallest detail caught their eye, such as an unusual clasp on a belt, but above all they excelled in capturing the individual expressions of the men who were the live models of the terracotta warriors.

The hands and heads of the warriors, and the tails and forelocks of the horses, were made and fired separately, then attached with clay strips. What is so arresting about the portraiture is the fact that each head is an individual study. To suggest that the different faces represent types rather than actual people, as some Western scholars have done, is to miss the point: Zheng's anxiety about the after-life drove him to recruit into the terracotta army only the spirits of the men whom he totally could trust.

The 1980 discovery of the bronze chariot pit, seventeen metres from the western edge of the tumulus, stirred up controversy about the mausoleum site. It has encouraged the view that the First Emperor's tomb might be similarly undisturbed by the rebels. No one knows if this is the case, although preliminary surveys of the tumulus have not uncovered any positive evidence of pillage. The bronze chariots themselves are somewhat less than actual size, but the 3,000 components used for each vehicle exhibit a high level of craftsmanship in the casting, welding, soldering and drilling.

Other finds near to the tumulus, on the western side between the inner and outer walls, include 31 small pits containing the skeletons of rare animals and birds; they are accompanied by kneeling terracotta figures. Beyond the outer wall, on the eastern side, another 91 pits have also been located. These appear to contain the imperial stables, as bones of horses are found there in addition to terracotta guards and grooms. But to the south-west, however, are the most chilling remains, for here are the graves of many of the conscripts who laboured at Mount Li.

Given the apparent scale of the First Emperor's determination – of which the leg-irons of the conscripts bear witness – there is every reason to expect that archaeologists will eventually discover most of the things that an absolute ruler considered indispensable in the after-life. All that we can do in the West is admire the infinite patience with which Chinese archaeologists are exploring his burial place.

Elaborate hairstyles of the terracotta warriors.

*Excavation in Pit
No. 2.*

THE FALL OF THE QIN DYNASTY

The quarrel in 212 B.C. between the First Emperor and Fu Su, his eldest son, probably sealed the fate of the dynasty. The blank refusal of the haunted ruler to listen to the advice of the crown prince meant that only an inner circle of advisers could have any influence on affairs of state, especially when the eastern provinces were being exhaustively toured in search of the elixir of life. For daring to speak out about the execution of dissident scholars, Fu Su was banished from the court and therefore unable to thwart the conspiracy of Li Si and the eunuch Zhao Gao on the First Emperor's death in 210 B.C. He was forced, along with general Meng Tian, to commit suicide.

The Grand Councillor and the Grand Eunuch were driven to remove Fu Su from the political scene by a belief that their own lives were at stake. Identified with the extreme policies of the First Emperor and conscious of the earlier end of Shang Yang, these two men conspired to elevate Hu Hai as the Second Emperor, even though it was transparent that he lacked any real ability. A creature of Zhao Gao, the twenty-one year old Second Emperor, Ershi Huangdi, proved incapable of ruling with any consistency and in nervousness he struck down all who opposed him. "Ten of the princes of the imperial family," the Histories note, "were torn limb from limb." The guiding hand of Zhao Gao can be seen behind these purges, which claimed even Li Si in 208 B.C., for the eunuch was preparing his own bid for supreme power. In the ensuing year Zhao Gao compelled the Second Emperor to commit suicide, but the Histories explain

when Zhao Gao hung the imperial tally from his belt and ascended into the audience chamber, no official would accept his usurpation, and three persons there offered him harm. Realizing that Heaven had refused to grant him the empire, and that the officials would not co-operate with his desire, he summoned the nephew of the First Emperor and handed over the government to him.

By 207 B.C., however, it was too late for the dynasty: China was already in the throes of its first national revolt.

Court intrigue had given the oppressed Chinese people a chance to throw off the Qin yoke. They were enraged by the excessive burden of forced labour on public works, in particular the Great Wall and extravagant buildings in and around Xianyang; the enforced movements of population to newly conquered territories in the far north and the extreme south; the cruelty of the legal code; and the rude ending of the old feudal order. The rebellion had been started in 209 B.C. by a poor farmhand named Chen Sheng, who lived in the Yangzi river valley. Although his initial rising was crushed, the general dislike of Qin restriction swiftly produced a popular movement throughout the provinces, against which neither the Second Emperor nor his hapless successor had any hope of success. The rebels effectively destroyed Qin in 206 B.C. but not until four years afterwards was Liu Bang able to found the succeeding Han dynasty.

Yet so thorough were the changes that the First Emperor had made that all attempts to re-establish the feudal states which had existed prior to 221 B.C. failed. As a result the early Han rulers settled for a compromise between local and central government, granting a limited number of fiefs to members of the imperial house as well as certain old feudal households, but these diminished holdings were intertwined with districts controlled by officials. There was no going back to the feudalism which the First Emperor's army had destroyed, for dreadful though the fifteen years of the Qin rule were, they had shaped a political structure that would last China for two millennia. The enduring achievement of Zheng was the unification of China as an empire.

FURTHER READING

In English there are unfortunately few books on the Qin dynasty. The titles listed here should therefore be seen as a general way of approaching what is a most fascinating period of Chinese history.

Bai Shouyi   *An Outline History of China*, Beijing, 1982.

Bodde, D.   *China's First Unifier. A Study of the Ch'in (Qin) dynasty as seen in the Life of Li Ssu (Li Si) (c.280–208 B.C.)*, Leiden 1938; reprinted Hong Kong 1967.
                   "The state and empire of Ch'in" (Qin) in *The Cambridge History of China, Volume One*, (eds.) D. Twitchett and J. K. Fairbank, Cambridge, 1986.

de Bary, W. T.   *Sources of Chinese Tradition, Volume One*, New York, 1960.

Burton, W.   *Records of the Historian* (Sima Qian), New York, 1958.

Cotterell, A.   *The First Emperor of China*, London and New York, 1981.

Fitzgerald, C. P.   *China. A Short Cultural History*, London, 1935.

Hsu Cho-yun   *Ancient China in Transition. An Analysis of Social Mobility, 722–222 B.C.*, Stamford, 1965.

Rubin, V. A.   *Individual and State in Ancient China. Essays on Four Chinese Philosophers; Confucius, Mo Tzu, Shang Yang and Chuang Tzu*, trans. S. I. Levene, New York, 1976.

*Armoured soldie
(right)*

*Armoured
infantryman, who
once held a halberd.*

74

A model of a Qin chariot, reconstructed from impressions found in the soil at Mount Li.

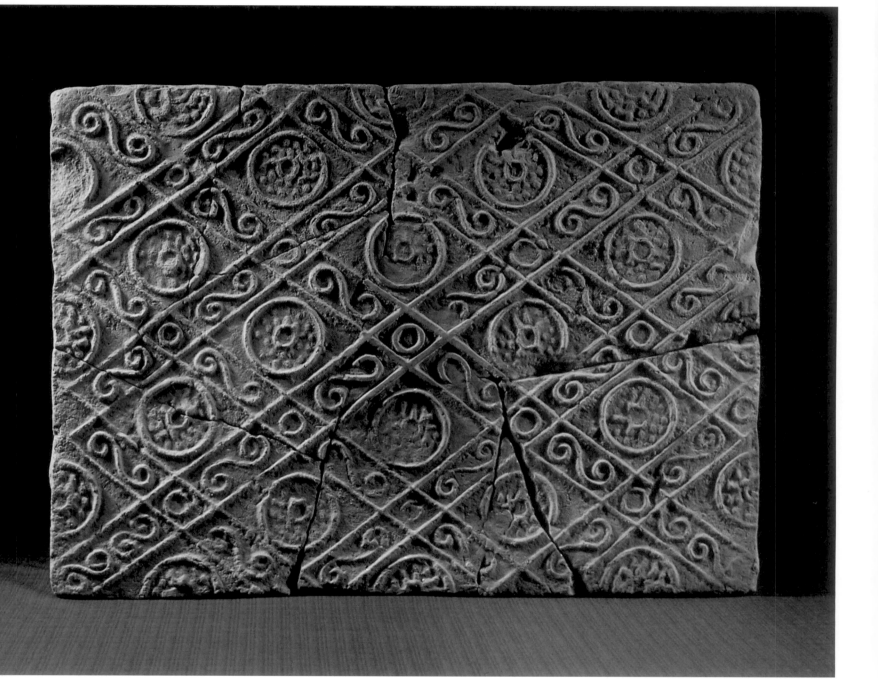

Broken grey brick excavated from the Xianyang palace. It was used for paving floors.

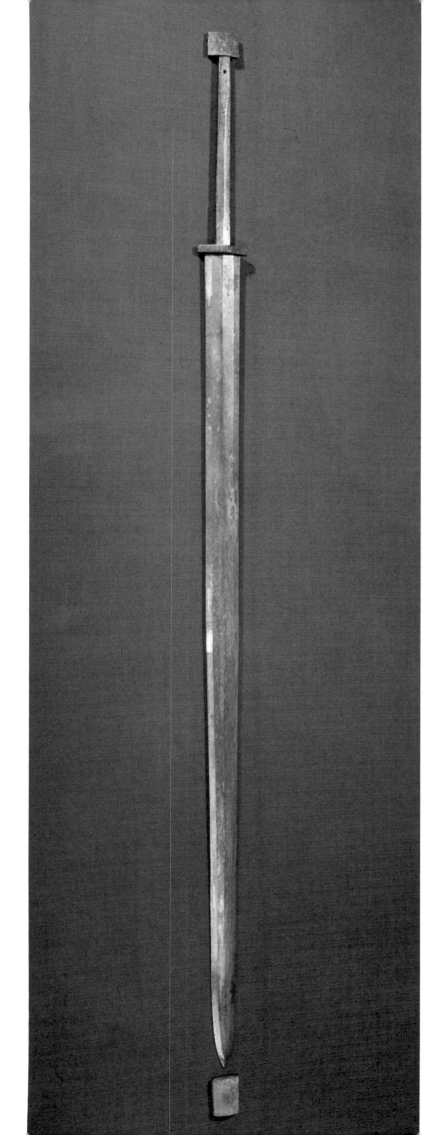

Bronze sword
excavated in May
1981 from Pit No. 1.
Surprisingly it was
found to be sharp, a
result of the
chromium involved
in its manufacture.

A bronze crossbow
mechanism and
crossbow bolts as
found in Pit No. 1.

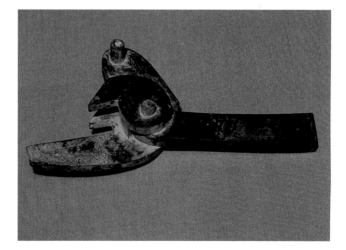

77

A standard measure. Under the First Emperor weights and measures were strictly standardised.

A five-sided terracotta water pipe with a string-like pattern on the exterior surface.

Solid grey pottery brick from the floor of Pit No. 1. It carries the maker's mark (below), since under Qin law he was held personally responsible for its quality of manufacture.

*Hollow brick with
incised dragon
design, unearthed
at the Xianyang
palace.*

A Qin pottery vessel.

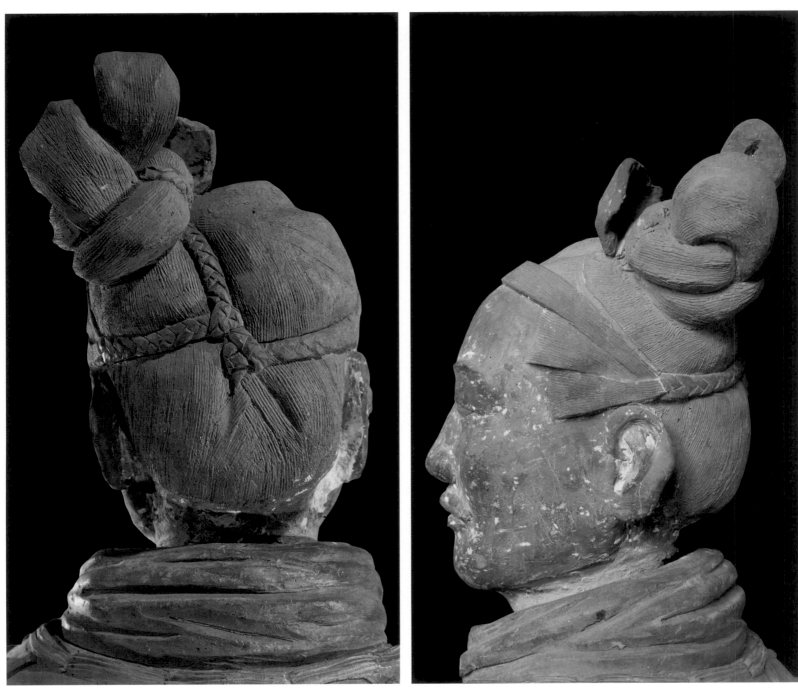

Elaborate hairstyles are common amongst the warriors of the terracotta army.

Hand of an
unarmoured soldier.
Hands and heads
were modelled
separately.

83

*Grey brick with
impressed design,
found at the
Xianyang palace.*

Archaeologists at
work in a corridor
of Pit No. 1.

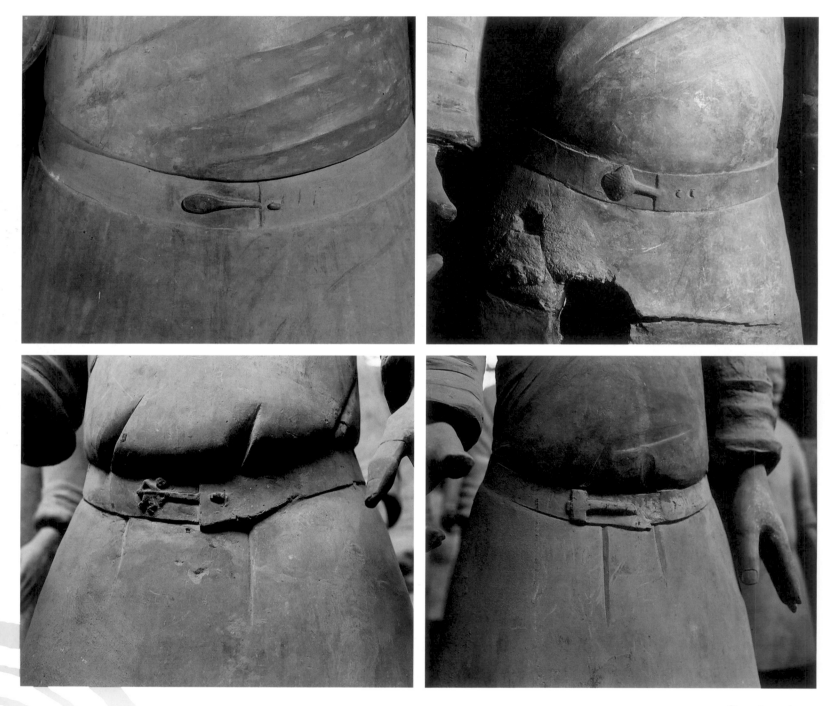

Qin potter-sculptors had an eye for detail: here are four distinct belt hooks belonging to unarmoured warriors.

*A chariot horse
from Pit No. 1.*

*Unarmoured
crossbowman from
Pit No. 1.*

*Chariot horses
standing next to the
remains of a
wooden chariot.*

89

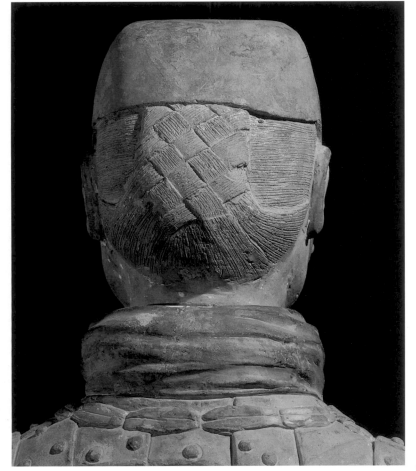

Hairstyle of an armoured cavalryman from Pit No. 2.

Two tile ends, excavated in 1976 at Mount Li.

One of the sev designs of arm found amongs terracotta arm This officer ro a chariot. (rig

Grey pressed brick
discovered at
Mount Li.

A tile end of typical
Qin design.

*Senior Qin officer,
possibly a general.
The decorative
bows indicate rank.*

Standing crossbowman from the vanguard of Pit No. 1.

Kneeling terracotta stableboy found near the First Emperor's tumulus in 1964.

Iron implement found near the graves of the conscripts who built Mount Li.

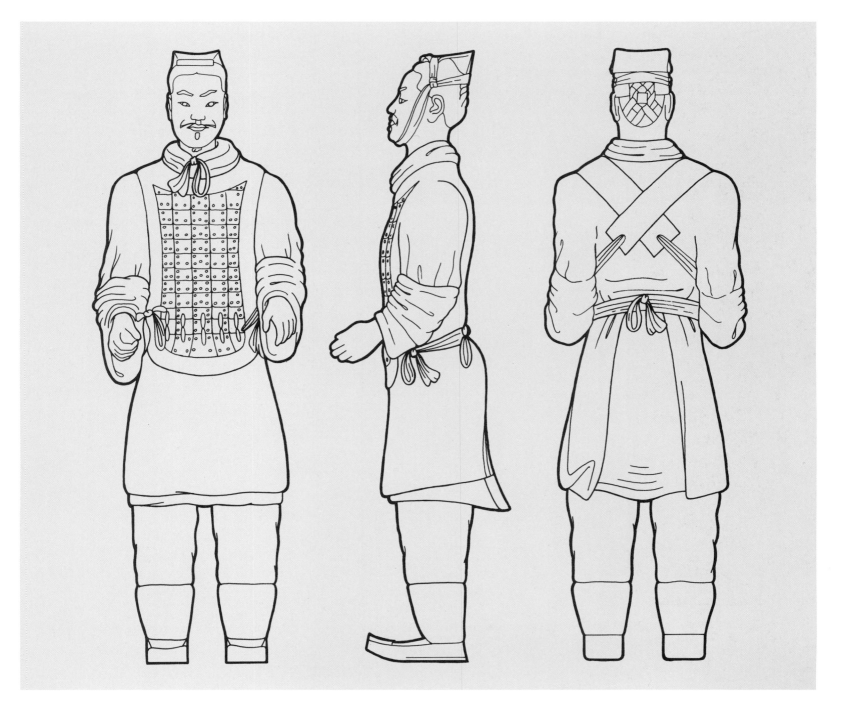

*Charioteer from Pit
No. 2.*

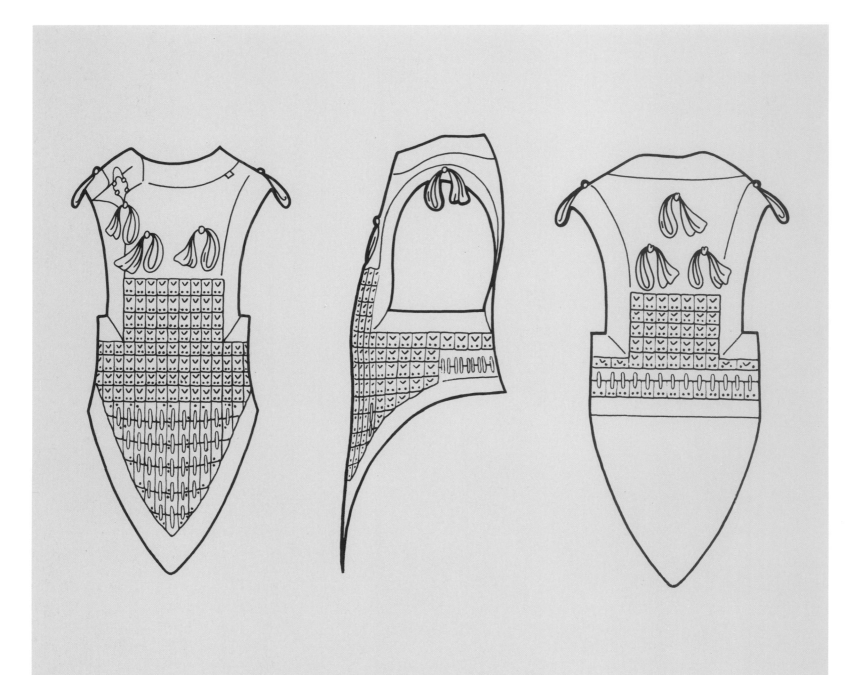

Detail of the armour of a high ranking Qin officer.

*Infantry armour
from Pit No. 1.*

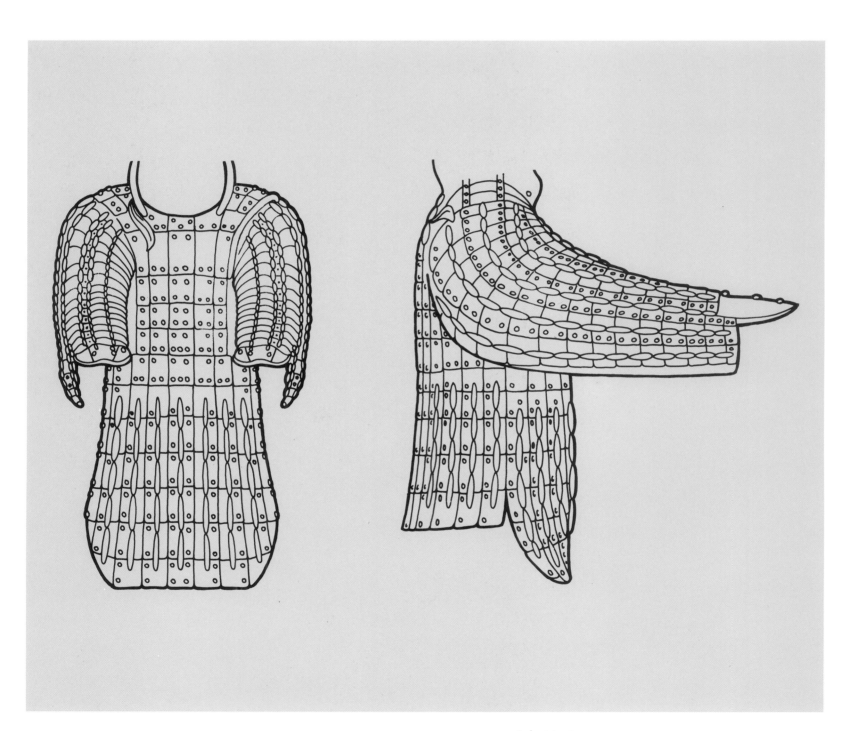

A charioteer's armour afforded complete protection for the arms.

Kneeling
crossbowman. Note
the elaborate way
in which his hair
has been dressed.

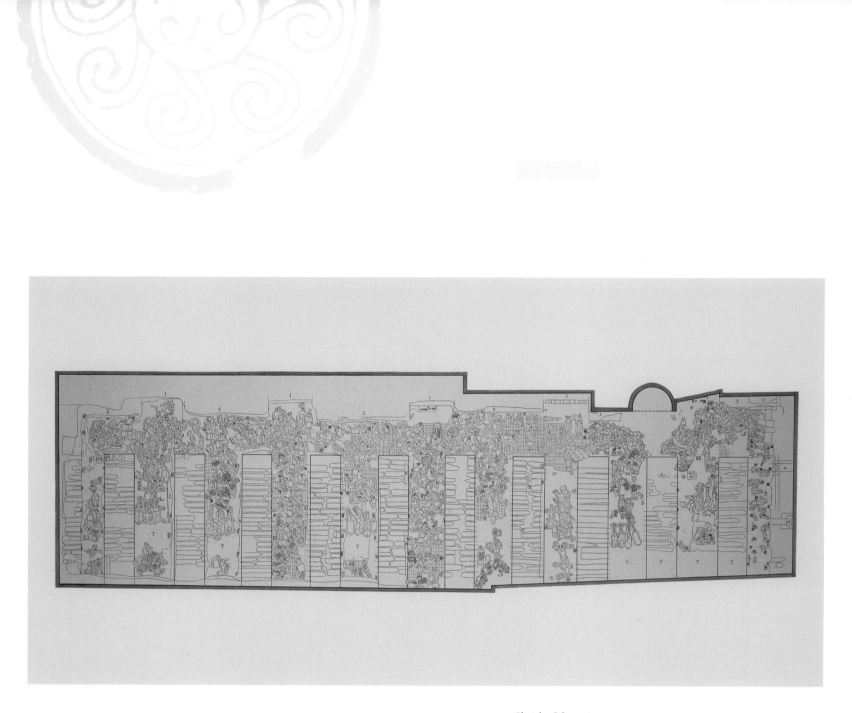

Sketch of the east end of Pit No. 1, on excavation.

INDEX

Kneeling crossbowman from Pit No. 2.